D1285617

THE LEGO® GAMES BOOK

Written by Tori Kosara

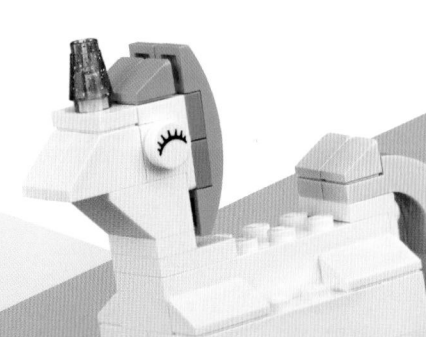

DK

CONTENTS

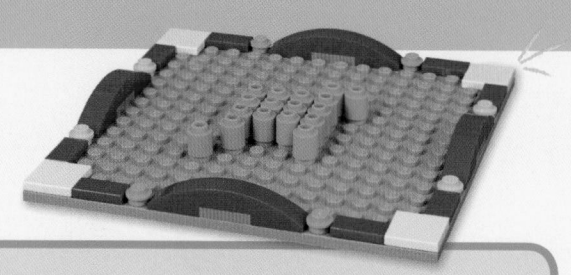

WHISPER IT

Trying to hear a whispered word can lead to funny results. Let a friend whisper a building idea to you and see whether you can make the correct model. This game starts out quietly, but it might end in loud laughter!

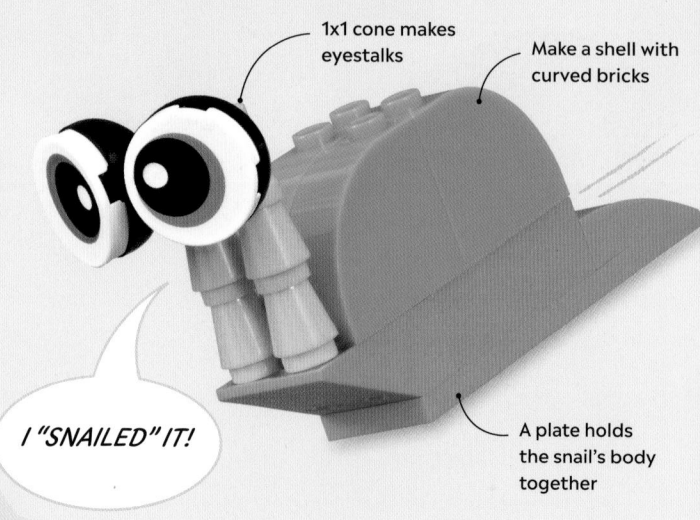

1x1 cone makes eyestalks

Make a shell with curved bricks

A plate holds the snail's body together

I "SNAILED" IT!

Tooth plate looks like the parrot's feathers

VS.

Plate with clip for a foot

I SAID CARROT, NOT PARROT!

How to play

1 One player writes down a building idea and hides it. The same player whispers the idea to another player just once in their quietest voice.

2 The builder must make a model of what they think they've heard. It's not as easy as you might think!

3 When the builder is finished, check the paper to see whether the model is correct. If it is, the builder wins. If not, then the whisperer wins.

TIC-TAC-TOE

This classic game has been given a fun LEGO® twist! Who will be the first to get three pieces in a row? You can be Team Hot Dog or Team Popcorn, or use any other wacky pieces you have.

Rows can be horizontal, vertical, or diagonal

2x2 jumper plate holds game pieces in place

Attach an ice-cream scoop to a 1x1 brick to make popcorn

BET YOU CAN'T "KETCHUP" WITH ME!

Tiles make a colorful border

Make the base with plates

Game pieces can be any small elements you have

How to play

1 Build a board with nine squares. Create the squares using jumper plates in the center of each square.

2 Choose or build five game pieces of one design for one player and five of a different design for the other player.

3 Take turns placing a game piece on the board. The winner is the first person to get three of their pieces in a row.

UNSTICK THE BRICKS

LEGO pieces are designed to stick together. This simple game challenges you to do the opposite! Try it for yourself and find out just how tricky it can be to pry one LEGO piece away from another.

TOP TIP
You can play with LEGO plates of any size, but remember—the smaller the plate, the harder the challenge will be!

THIS IS HARDER THAN IT LOOKS!

2x4 plate

VS.

How to play

1 Find two LEGO plates of the same size—2x3 or 2x4 plates work best for this game. Then stick them together.

2 Ask a friend to hold one plate while you hold the other and try to pull them apart with one hand each. Can you do it in 10 seconds?

Level up
Once you're a pro at unsticking the plates with one hand each, try doing it with gloves on, then mittens. Will you be able to pull the plates apart?

BRICK COUNTDOWN

All you need for this game is 20 bricks—and a little imagination. The challenge is to build something with fewer and fewer bricks. It's amazing what you can build with a small amount of pieces!

2x4 wedge plate makes a sail

How to play

1 Gather 20 LEGO pieces. Try to make sure there is a good mix of elements.

2 Build a model using all 20 LEGO pieces. Next, take apart the model. Remove one piece and set it aside. With 19 pieces, make a completely new mini build.

3 Keep taking away one piece after you've finished each model until you have just one brick left.

This ship uses all 20 pieces

This elephant is made with 11 elements

Plate with bar looks like an elephant's trunk

Will this slope make it to the next round?

Brick with side studs

Just three pieces make a hammer

TOP TIP

Think small! With 20 pieces, you will be able to build only small models. Consider how each small piece can represent something bigger.

BEAT THE CLOCK

Three, two, one—build! You need a steady hand to build against the clock in this fast-paced game. Challenge your family and friends to find out who can build a model at rocket speed.

How to play

1 Choose a simple model idea for all the players to build.

2 Set a timer for 30 seconds.

3 The first player to complete the model in 30 seconds is the winner.

TOP TIP

Your chosen model doesn't have to be a rocket. It can be a cake, a snake, or anything else that can be built easily in a short amount of time.

HEY—NOT SO FAST!

1x1 brick with side stud

Rocket engine piece

Antenna makes the tip of the rocket

1x1 cone

Joystick

1x2 plate with clip

Launchpad stand is made by stacking pieces

Level up

If one build is too easy, try adding on to your first model in the next round. Give players 30 seconds to build something else, such as a launchpad for a rocket ship.

Keep the builds steady on plates

BUILD AND REBUILD

Say cheese! Grab your camera and get ready to put your building skills—and your memory—to the test. Can you recreate a model using just a photograph?

LOOK, MOM—I'M ON CAMERA!

Eyes attach to bricks with side studs

Make a robot hand with a curved slope

Arm is a 1x2 plate with bar

Disassembled model pieces

A small plate stops the model from falling over

1x1 brick with side stud

How to play

1 Build a simple model, such as a robot, and take a photo.

2 Break your model apart. Then try to rebuild the model using just the photograph.

PUZZLE CUBE

This cool cube is actually made up of seven different brick-built shapes. They all slot together to make one puzzle. Build each shape and then challenge your friends to solve this baffling brainteaser.

Figure out how each shape will fit into the other before you build

SOLVED IT!

Use one color for each different shape

THIS IS A REAL PUZZLE!

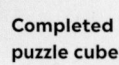

Completed puzzle cube

Puzzle pieces

These are the shapes you need to build in order to make your cube.

How to build

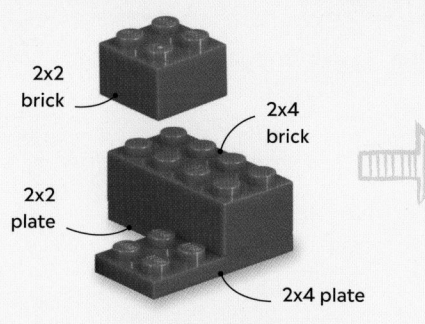

2x2 brick

2x4 brick

2x2 plate

2x4 plate

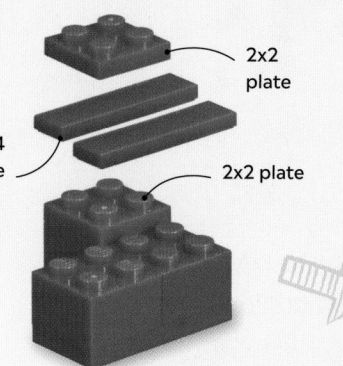

2x2 plate

1x4 tile

2x2 plate

2x2 tile

2x2 brick

1 Plates make a sturdy base. Use larger bricks to create the angles you need to achieve each shape.

2 Plates help add a little bit of height to the shape.

3 Finish the shape by covering it with tiles. Make sure all the parts of each shape are the same color.

Completed shape

4 Now that this shape is finished, build the rest.

TOP TIP
Cover each shape with tiles so that no studs are showing. This way, the shapes will fit together without getting stuck.

Solve it!
If you're stumped, follow these steps to put the puzzle cube together.

1

Shape slots into the center of the cube

2

3

4

ONE-TYPE-OF-BRICK CHALLENGE

The cute models on this page are made using pieces that are all the same size—1x2 bricks. What can you build using just one kind of LEGO brick?

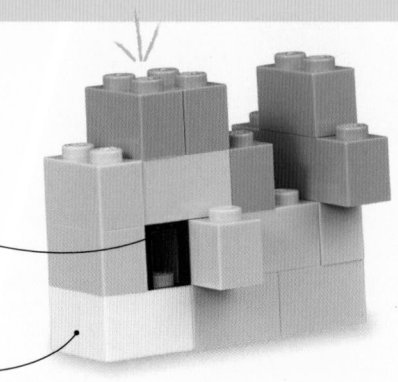

1x2 transparent brick makes an eye for the whale

A different color makes a clear mouth

Stack bricks in the opposite direction to form the llama's snout

Use any color bricks

How to play

1 Sort your bricks into piles by type. For example, make a pile of 1x2 bricks and a pile of 1x4 plates.

2 Choose one size of brick to build with. The bricks can be any color as long as they are the same size and shape.

3 Get creative and see how many models you can build using one kind of brick. Will your friends and family be able to guess what you've made?

This stack forms a snail shell

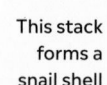

WHICH SIZE BRICK WILL I FIND?

SPIN IT TO WIN IT!

Get ready for a spinning battle! Build a spinning top that can knock your opponents' LEGO tops right off the table. Play against friends and family to find out who will come out on top. Just try not to get dizzy!

LEGO Technic axle

2x2 round brick with axle hole

LEGO® Technic ball joint

TOP TIP
You can decorate your top however you like. Just make sure all sides have an equal weight so that it can spin.

Decorate your top with small elements

Dome

How to play

1 Everyone builds a top like this one. Decorate yours however you want.

2 Set the tops on a clear, flat surface like a table. Everyone spins their top at the same time.

3 The aim of the game is to knock your opponents' tops off the surface. Play as many rounds as you need until there is just one top left.

4 The player with their spinning top left last on the surface is the winner.

SOLVE A SUDOKU

Boggle your mind with a fun puzzle! Instead of using numbers, like most sudokus, use your LEGO bricks to play. It might be tricky at first, but practice makes perfect, so build lots of different sudokus to solve.

TOP TIP
Make sure your five game pieces look very different from each other to avoid getting them mixed up.

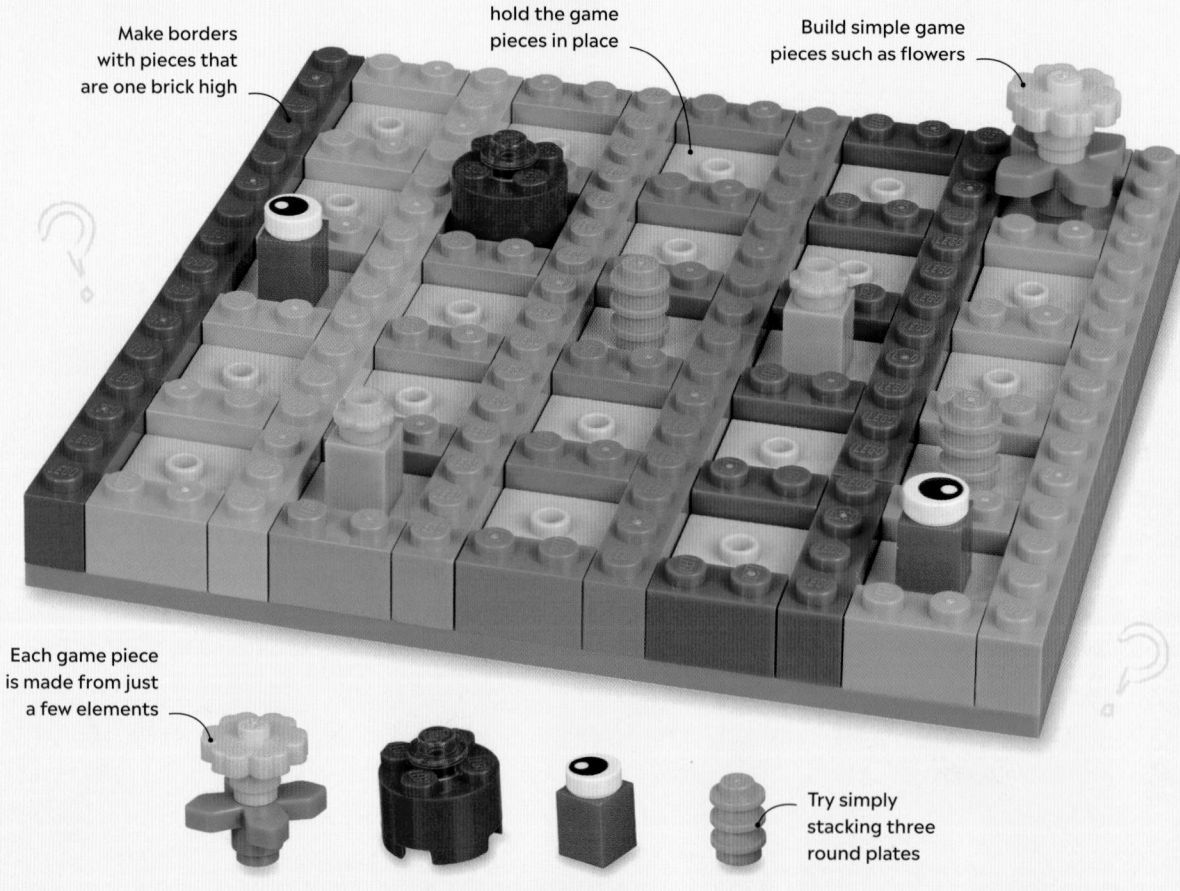

Jumper plates hold the game pieces in place

Make borders with pieces that are one brick high

Build simple game pieces such as flowers

Each game piece is made from just a few elements

Try simply stacking three round plates

Game pieces

How to build

2x2 jumper plate

2x2 plate

16x16 baseplate

Use different colors to mark each row

1 Find a large baseplate to form the base of the game board.

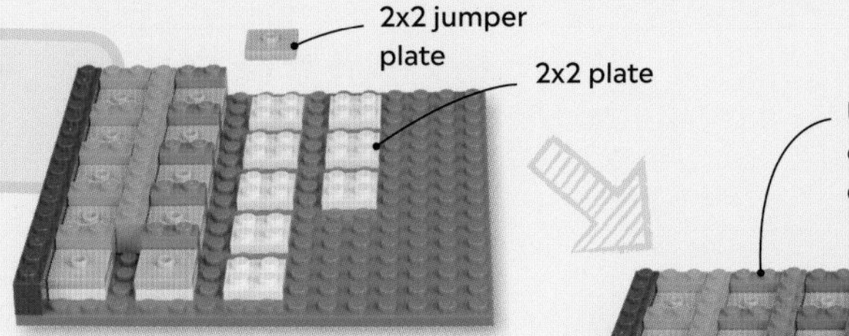

2 Build the 25 boxes needed to complete the grid. Leave one row of studs between each box.

3 Complete the boxes and separate each space with a 1x2 brick. Next, make five of each game piece.

This sudoku board is ready!

Just one of each game piece is in every row and column

How to play

1 The aim of the puzzle is to fill the grid with the game pieces, using one of each of the different game pieces in every row and column.

2 What makes it really tricky is that you can't use any game piece twice in any row or column!

3 Start filling out the grid, checking each row and column as you go. You may have to try lots of different combinations before solving a sudoku puzzle—it's all part of the process!

19

You might have played charades before, but how about trying it with LEGO bricks? Instead of testing your acting talents, this game tests your building skills. Can the other players guess what your scene is supposed to be?

How to play

1 Write down phrases, actions, or the names of books or movies on small pieces of paper. Put them in a container.

2 Each player randomly chooses a slip of paper, making sure that no one else can see what's written on it.

3 Using LEGO elements, everyone builds a small scene that describes whatever is written on their paper.

4 After the models have been built, everyone takes turns guessing what each scene is. Don't give any clues. Whoever guesses correctly first wins.

WELL, THIS IS A WALK IN THE PARK.

Be sure to add minifigures to help "act" out the scene

"Going for a walk"

The carrot is a good clue

"Gardening"

Transparent pieces make good bubbles

"Taking a bath"

PIZZA DELIVERY

Cook up some fun with a LEGO pizza-making competition. Could you whip up a pepperoni pizza with mushrooms and extra cheese in just 20 seconds? There's only one way to find out—may the best chef win!

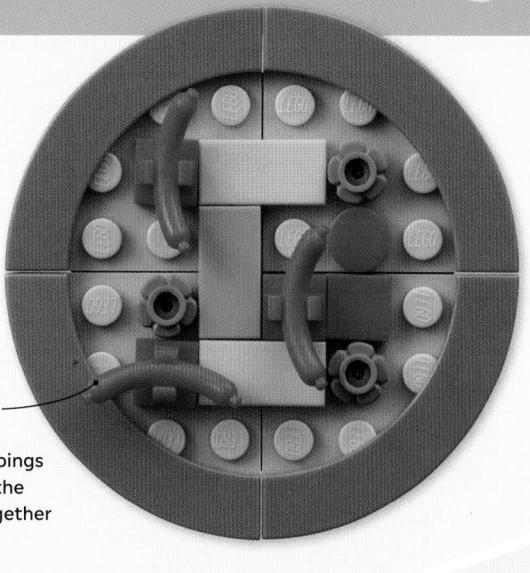

4x4 curved tile is a crust

Hot dogs are handy when the customer asks for sausage

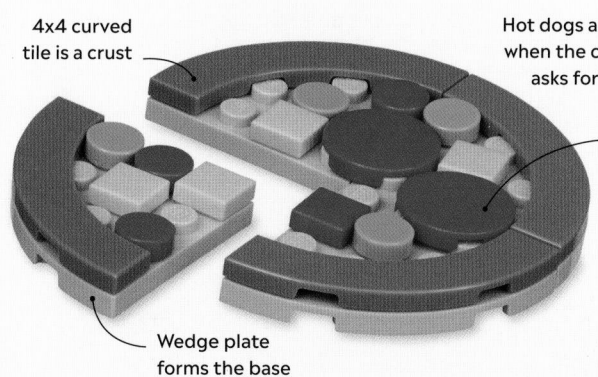

Use toppings to hold the base together

Wedge plate forms the base

Flower element for a green pepper

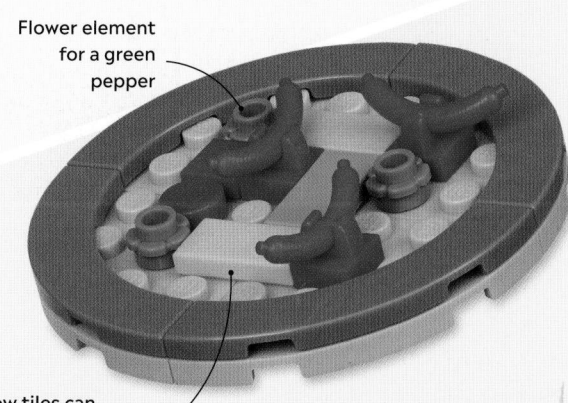

How to play

1 Make a base for each chef. For each round, decide who will be the customer.

2 Place a pile of food pieces and small LEGO elements where all of the chefs can reach them.

3 Set a timer for 20 seconds. The customer shouts out pizza toppings and the chefs must try to make a pizza that looks like the order. The best-looking pizza wins!

Yellow tiles can be cheese or pineapple

I'D LIKE A "PIZZA" THE ACTION!

SHAKE UP YOUR SENSES

Can you tell what a LEGO model is, using only your hands? Put your sense of touch to the test by guessing what your friends' models are with just your fingers as your guide. No peeking!

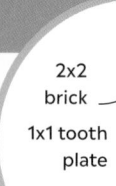

2x2 brick

1x1 tooth plate

How to play

1 One player wears a blindfold while the others set a timer for five minutes.

2 The builders have five minutes to make one mini model each.

3 When time is up, the blindfolded player guesses what each player has built by feeling the models. If the blindfolded player guesses correctly, they win. If they don't, then the builders win.

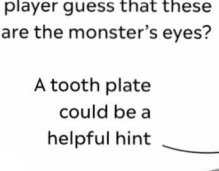

Will the blindfolded player guess that these are the monster's eyes?

A tooth plate could be a helpful hint

Slopes could feel like wings or arms

Wheels are a good clue that this is a monster truck

Level up

For an extra challenge, let the blindfolded player use just one finger to feel the models when the builders have finished. It will be very tricky to guess what mini builds the builders have created!

TEST YOUR MEMORY

Just a handful of LEGO elements is all you need for a fun memory challenge. Put your friends to the test to find out who can remember the most pieces.

TOP TIP

Try saying the names of the elements to yourself as you look at them. It might help you remember them more quickly.

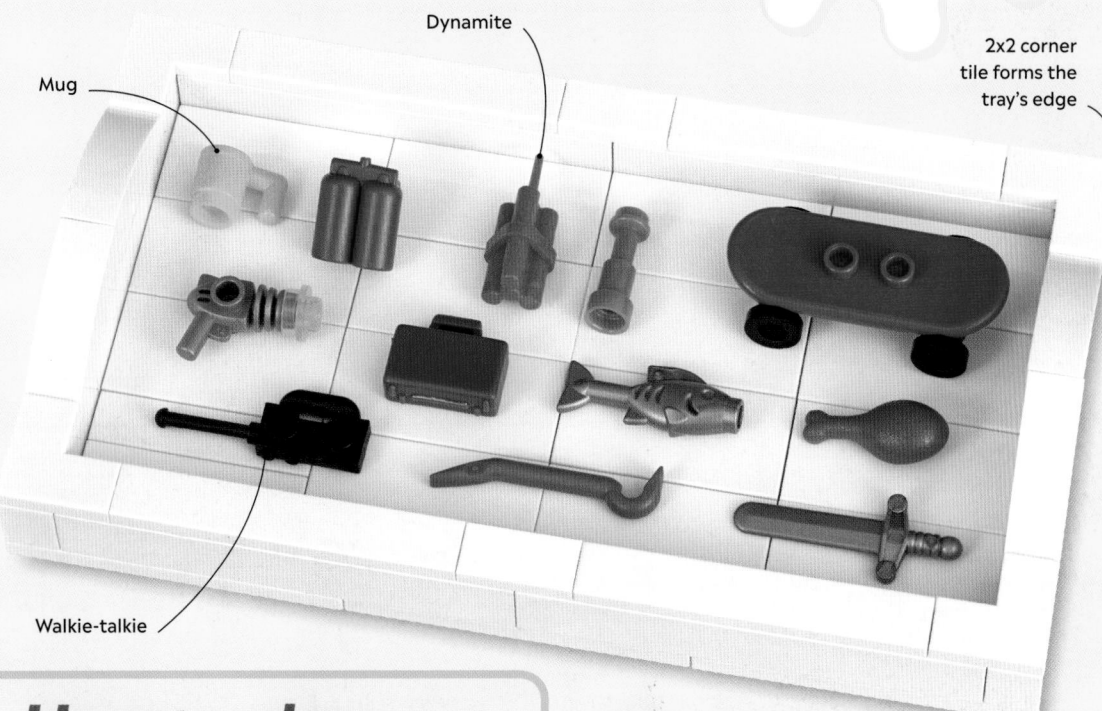

Dynamite

Mug

2x2 corner tile forms the tray's edge

Walkie-talkie

How to play

1 Lay out up to 20 LEGO elements on a flat surface. Give all players 30 seconds to look at the pieces. Then cover them with a dish towel or a piece of paper.

2 Set a timer for 60 seconds. Each player must try to correctly list all of the elements before time is up. The player who writes down the most correct elements wins.

23

TEASE YOUR BRAIN

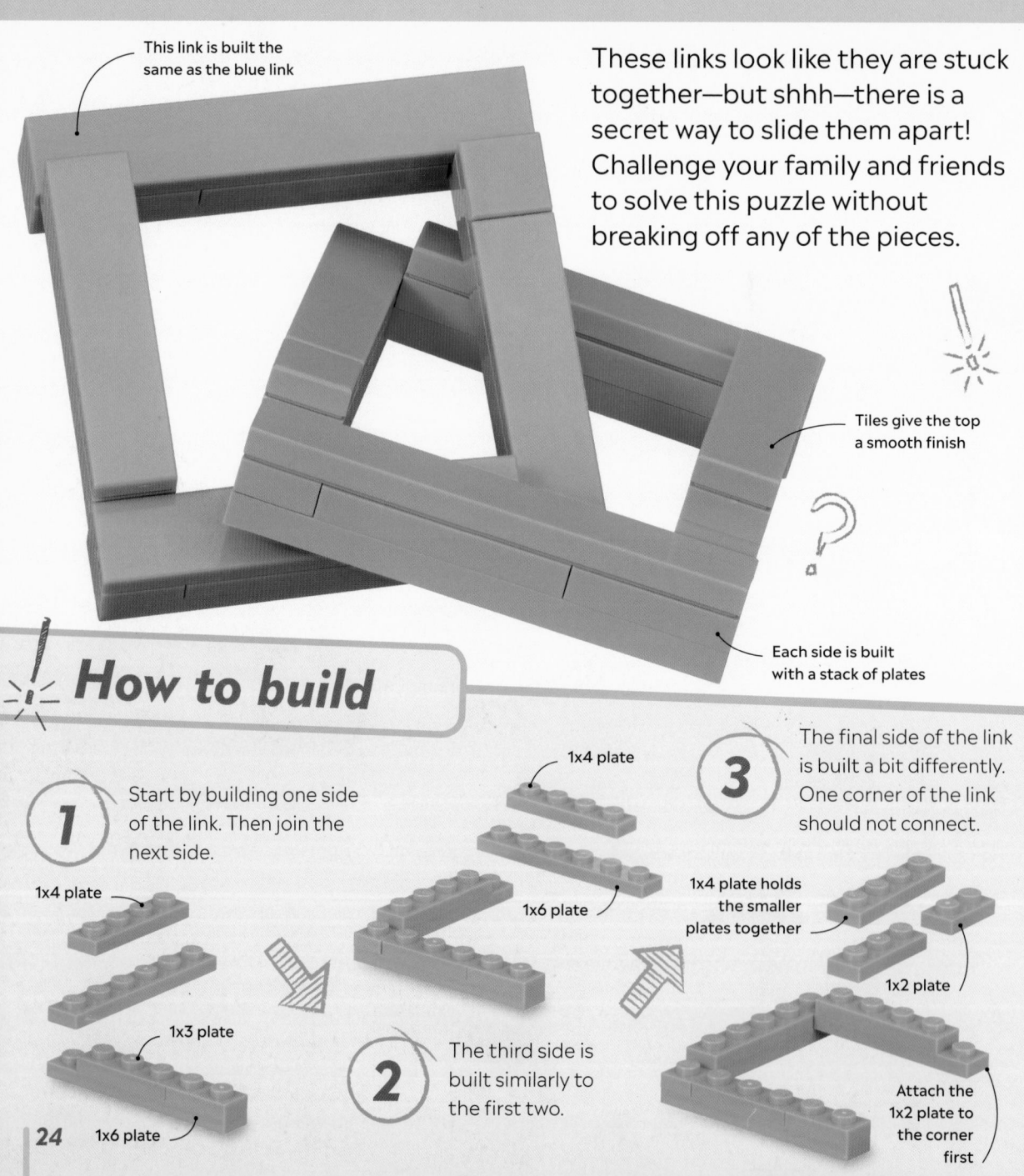

This link is built the same as the blue link

These links look like they are stuck together—but shhh—there is a secret way to slide them apart! Challenge your family and friends to solve this puzzle without breaking off any of the pieces.

Tiles give the top a smooth finish

Each side is built with a stack of plates

How to build

1 Start by building one side of the link. Then join the next side.

1x4 plate

1x3 plate

1x6 plate

2 The third side is built similarly to the first two.

1x4 plate

1x6 plate

3 The final side of the link is built a bit differently. One corner of the link should not connect.

1x4 plate holds the smaller plates together

1x2 plate

Attach the 1x2 plate to the corner first

Open
corner

Open
corner

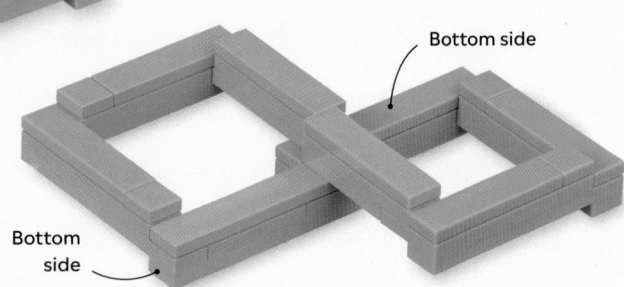

Bottom side

Bottom
side

1 Hold your links so that the open corners are facing each other.

2 Gently slide the corners together so that the links connect. It helps to line up the bottom sides of each link.

Both links are
connected

3 Ask your family and friends to get the links apart without breaking off any pieces. See whether they can solve this tricky brainteaser!

WHO CAN SOLVE IT IN THE QUICKEST TIME?

This plate does
not connect to
the one below it

5 Cover all the studs with tiles. Then make the second link in exactly the same way.

Attach tiles
to plates

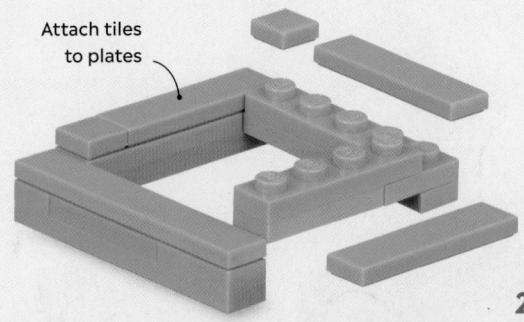

4 Start covering the link with tiles.

25

GUESS THE NUMBER

Will anyone be able to guess how many LEGO bricks are in your container? Fill up a transparent cup or jar with LEGO elements and ask everyone how many pieces they think are inside. The closest guess wins the game!

Level up

Set a 10-second "guessing" time limit for each player. The ticking clock will force players to make their best guesses very quickly.

Fill the container with as many pieces as you want

How to play

1 Count out a pile of bricks and write down the number on a piece of paper. Hide the paper so no one can see it.

2 Fill a transparent container with the LEGO pieces and ask your friends and family to guess how many are inside. Whoever gets the closest to the number you've written down is the winner.

Use a transparent container so your friends can see the pieces inside it

TRY NOT TO LAUGH

It can be hard to keep a straight face when you're looking at silly designs like this one. Challenge your friends to build the funniest prop and then find out who will have the last laugh.

Thin plates make sticks to hold up props

Slope looks like a waxed mustache

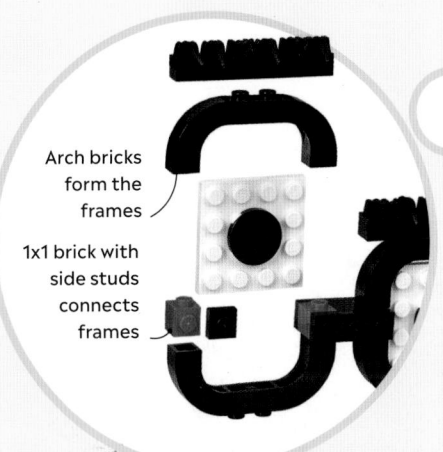

Arch bricks form the frames

1x1 brick with side studs connects frames

A big mustache might tickle your funny bone

Red bricks make a silly tongue

How to play

1 Build a prop that you can hold up to your face. Make it as big or as small as you like—it can be anything silly or funny.

2 Take turns holding your builds up to your faces. The last person to laugh wins the game!

WHO "NOSE" WHAT MAKES ME LAUGH?

TOP TIP

Before you build, think about things that your friends and family find funny. The aim of the game is to get them to laugh first!

27

ESCAPE THE MAZE

Can you find your way out of this labyrinth? Build a maze and then see whether you can guide a ball through the twists and turns in just 30 seconds. Watch out for the dead ends!

THIS GAME IS A-MAZE-ING!

32x32 baseplate

Passages need to be two or more studs wide for the ball to fit

How to play

1 Create your own maze with a large baseplate. Build the walls as high as you like, but make sure the passages are wide enough for the LEGO ball to fit through.

2 Make sure there are two open spaces—one entrance and one exit. Place the ball at the entrance to the maze and set a timer for 30 seconds.

3 Tilt the game board to try to move the ball through the maze passages from the entrance to the exit before time is up.

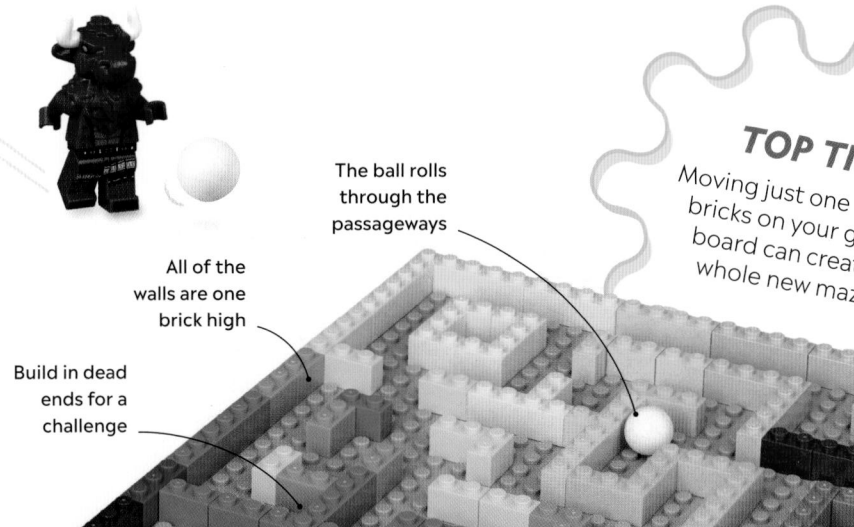

The ball rolls through the passageways

All of the walls are one brick high

Build in dead ends for a challenge

Try to get the ball to the maze's exit

TOP TIP
Moving just one or two bricks on your game board can create a whole new maze!

Place the ball here to start

Build maze walls with any colors

SPECIAL BRICK
This game uses a LEGO soccer ball. If you don't have this piece, you can use any other small ball, or trace your finger from start to finish.

I'M HAVING A BALL!

NO-THUMBS CHALLENGE

You need fast fingers for this building challenge. Can you build models like these—but without using your thumbs? Grab some bricks and give it a try.

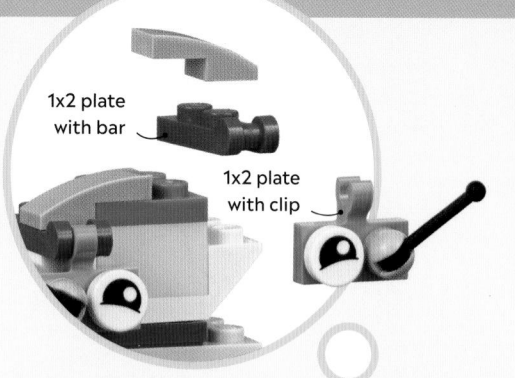

1x2 plate with bar

1x2 plate with clip

Curved slope for the head

Joystick makes a moving arm

THIS GAME GETS A THUMBS-UP!

Add eyes with printed tiles

Steering wheel is a spinning nose

Start with a plate and build upward

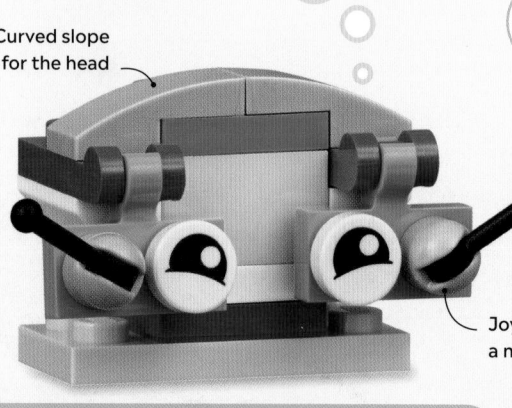

How to play

1 One person builds a small model, which the rest of the players must try to copy.

2 The other players try to build the same model—but without using their thumbs!

3 The first person to make the model without using their thumbs is the winner.

Level up

If this challenge is too easy, set a time limit for your build. You could set the clock for 60, 30, or even just 10 seconds!

30

THE FEWER, THE BETTER

Bigger isn't always better. In this game, the smallest model wins. Try to use as few bricks as possible to construct a recognizable little build like these houses.

TOP TIP

Think about recognizable shapes you can build with just a few bricks. What about an island with a palm tree?

Add white ice-cream scoops for chimney smoke

1x2 slope bricks make roof shingles

Flower elements form a garden

A small plate is a good start for micro builds

Walls can be made of any color bricks

How to play

Make window boxes with log pieces

Stacked headlight bricks look like window panes

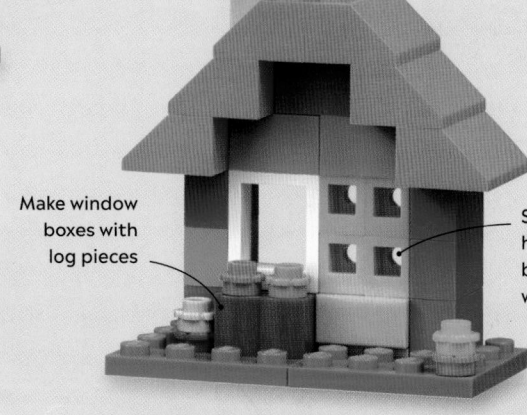

1 Together, decide on an object that all of the players will build. Each player makes a model of the agreed object.

2 Agree on some rules for the build. For example, these houses must have a roof, a window, and a window box with flowers.

3 The person who builds the object using the fewest bricks wins.

31

GO FOR A SPIN

In this game, players scramble to finish a model first. The catch is, each player can pick up only the bricks the spinner tells them to! Who will be the first to finish their build and win the game?

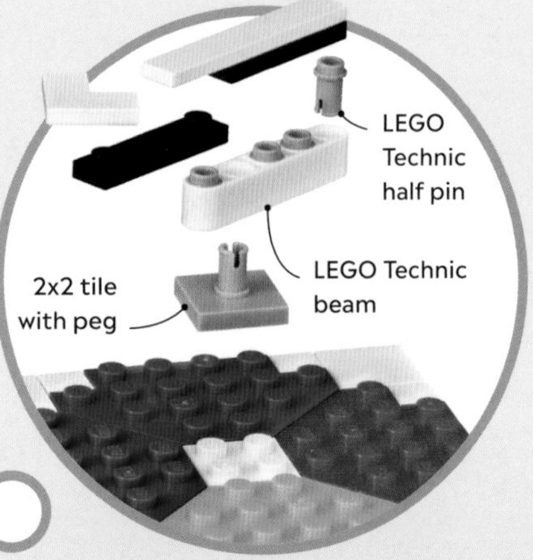

Get spinning

Build the spinner using a tile with a peg and a LEGO® Technic beam. Attach plates and tiles to the beam to make the arrow.

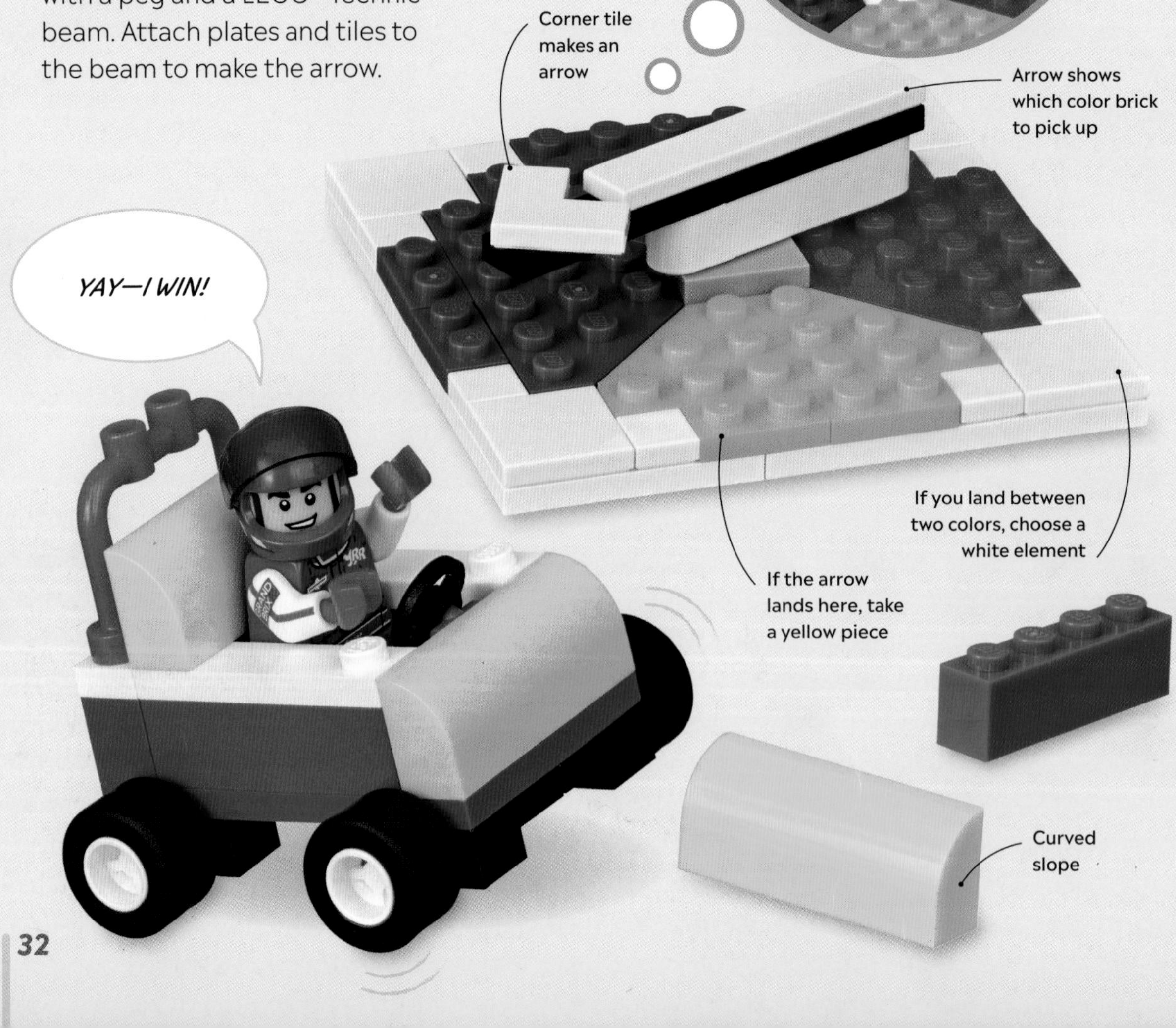

LEGO Technic half pin

2x2 tile with peg

LEGO Technic beam

Corner tile makes an arrow

Arrow shows which color brick to pick up

YAY—I WIN!

If you land between two colors, choose a white element

If the arrow lands here, take a yellow piece

Curved slope

Make a model

Before the game begins, one player must build a small model, such as this car. Everyone will take turns spinning the spinner to collect the bricks needed to build an identical model.

How to play

1 Start by building a spinner, with a spinnable arrow and four colored sections for the arrow to land on.

2 Next, one player builds a simple model, using only bricks that are the same color as the colors on the spinner. This is the model that the other players will replicate.

3 Each player takes a turn to spin the arrow. The player whose turn it is takes a LEGO element in the color the arrow points to after the spinner stops.

4 Start building the model, one brick at a time. Players might have to wait several spins before they can start putting the model together.

5 Take turns spinning until one player completes the model. The first player to finish wins.

Land on red to get this piece

Each player is given the wheels at the start of the game

1x4 tile with studs

The steering wheel is given out at the beginning of the game

I NEED TO LAND ON WHITE NEXT!

VS.

33

TOP THAT!

It's a race to the top in this stacking game. Challenge your friends to see how many bricks you can each stack up in 60 seconds. It sounds simple, but the tower has to stand on its own for another 60 seconds or you're out!

THE VIEW UP HERE IS GREAT!

How to play

1 Give each player the same number and size of bricks. Set a timer for 60 seconds and stack as many bricks as you can.

2x4 bricks make sturdy towers

I THINK I'M SCARED OF HEIGHTS!

2 When the timer stops, set it for another 60 seconds. Whoever has the tallest tower that is still standing is the winner.

You can stack bricks at any angle you want

Level up

Try building a tower with just one hand in 60 seconds. How high can you go?

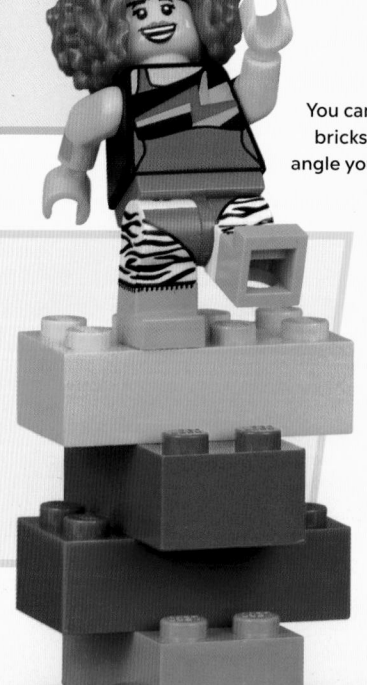

READ MY MIND

Test out your powers of telepathic communication to see whether you and a friend can build the same model using the same bricks. No peeking!

SPECIAL BRICK

Make a magical unicorn horn with a 1x1 transparent cone with glitter.

Top of the tail matches the other model

Matching horn placement

VS.

1x2 bricks make the feet of this unicorn

1x2 slope for a foot

Tails end with the same piece

THIS IS JUST LIKE MAGIC!

How to play

1 Set out an identical pile of bricks for each player. Sit back-to-back so you can't see the other model.

2 Name an object to build and set a timer for 10 minutes.

3 Without talking or looking at the other player's model, see whether you can build identical models before time is up.

4 If your models are the same, congratulations—you've read each other's mind!

35

PAINT A "BRICKTURE"

Show off your inner artist with a brick-built masterpiece. Challenge your family and friends to recreate a favorite piece of art, or even a photograph, using LEGO bricks. Ready, set, van Gogh!

The bold colors and straight lines look like abstract artist Piet Mondrian's work

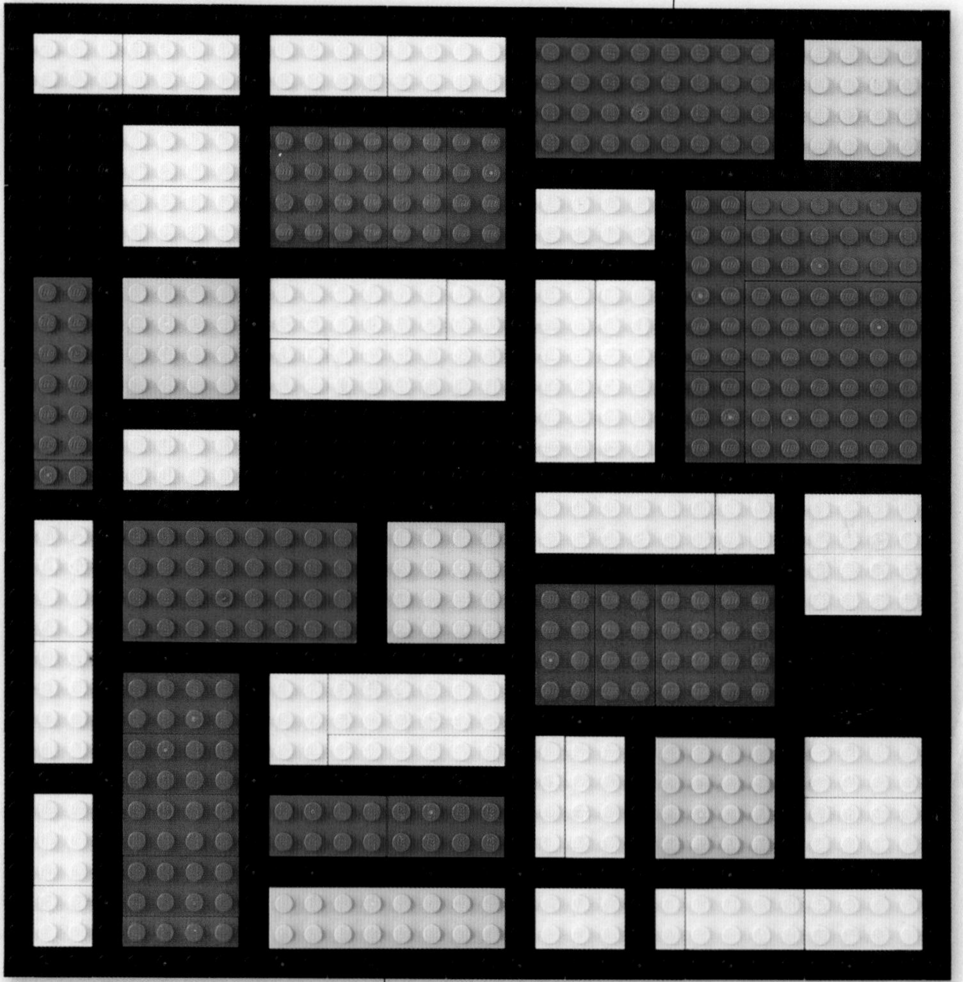

The height of the bricks is all the same to make a two-dimensional artwork

Taller elements give the artwork a three-dimensional effect

This brick-built artwork looks like Dutch painter Vincent van Gogh's *Sunflowers*

Build your artwork on plates like these

How to play

1 Find a family photograph or a famous work of art that you like.

2 Grab some bricks and try to recreate the artwork. You can build two-dimensionally or three-dimensionally.

3 When you're finished building, the other players must guess what you've recreated. The builder of the model with the most correct answers wins.

I'VE HAD A STROKE OF GENIUS.

PICK UP BRICKS

Chop, chop—the clock is ticking! Grab a pair of chopsticks or make some using LEGO bricks. Then see how many LEGO pieces you can pick up and move with your slippery sticks in 30 seconds.

How to play

1 Find a pair of chopsticks, or build some like these, and set out a pile of LEGO bricks.

2 Set a timer for 30 seconds and try to move as many bricks from the original pile to a new pile.

3 When time is up, count how many bricks you've moved. You get one point for each brick that is moved to the new pile.

Hold the chopsticks in one hand

Each stick is made of two layers of plates

PICK UP THE BRICKS— NOT ME!

The plates are covered with smooth tiles

Level up

If you're really good at this game, ban the bigger bricks! How many small elements can you pick up in 30 seconds?

Be sure you each have the same number of bricks in your starting pile if you're playing with a friend

BUILD ONE-HANDED

Can you win this challenge single-handedly? The models on this page were built using only one hand. Get your bricks ready and find out what you can build in 60 seconds with one hand behind your back.

How to play

1 Set out a pile of bricks on a flat surface.

2 Set a timer for one minute and put one hand behind your back. Start building with only one hand.

3 Whoever makes the most complete model using just one hand in 60 seconds is the winner.

Will you be able to stick eyes on with one hand?

WHERE ARE MY HANDS?

Start out with small simple builds like this one

Ice-cream scoop piece is easy to connect to a 1x1 round plate

Large piece forms a sturdy base

A baseplate will help keep your build stable

Connect bars and clips before adding them to a model

Level up

Switch hands! If you're right-handed, build with your left hand. If you're left-handed, try building with your right hand instead.

REVERSE IT

Let your building skills shine in this mirror-matching challenge. Can you figure out how to build the opposite half of one side of a LEGO model?

8x16 plate

Build one side of the model first

Tiles look like road markings

Plate with handle connects the wing to the body

Plate with clip

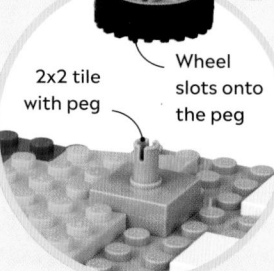

2x2 tile with peg

Wheel slots onto the peg

How to play

1 One player builds one side of a model. It can be as big or as small as you like.

2 The second player must build the other side of the model as a mirror image of the first side.

Level up

After you've mastered making flat mirror images, try three-dimensional building. Can you build identical butterfly wings?

BEAT IT TO THE FINISH LINE

Hatch a plan to make it across a racecourse without dropping your LEGO egg from your brick-built spoon. You can try this egg-cellent game on your own or grab some friends to see who can cross the finish line first.

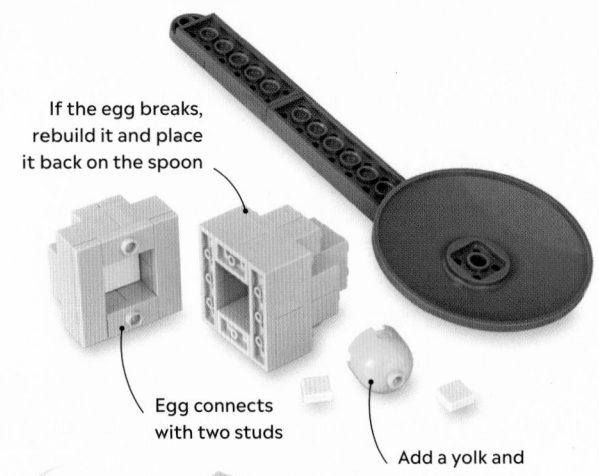

If the egg breaks, rebuild it and place it back on the spoon

Egg connects with two studs

Add a yolk and egg white

Layers of plates make the handle

Hold only the handle during the race

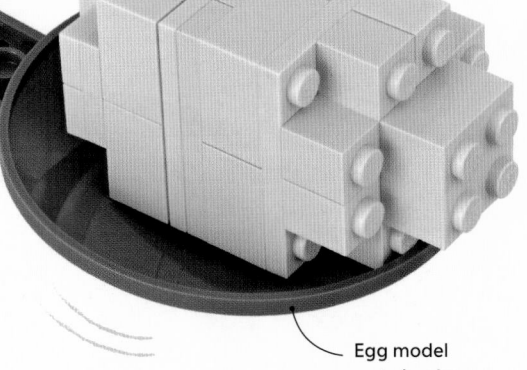

How to play

1 Build an egg and a spoon like these. Then place the egg on the wide part of the spoon.

2 Set a racecourse by marking a "start" and "finish" line. Then grab the handle of your spoon and race to the finish line.

3 If your egg falls off the spoon, you must start over. Whoever makes it over the finish line first with their egg still on the spoon is the winner!

Egg model rests in a large radar dish

I'M SO "EGG-CITED!"

41

CREATE CRAZY 'BOTS

These quirky robots each have their own cool names, jobs, and stories. Have you ever dreamed of building a robot that could do anything you want—like build you a tree house or squirt water on a hot day? Now is your chance to build any 'bot you want—the more creative, the better!

SPECIAL BRICK

The chain saw piece makes it clear right away that this robot must be some kind of builder.

HI! MY NAME IS SPARKY.

1x2 brick

1x2 grille

I'M FROM THE PLANET "BUILD-IT."

Head can rotate on 2x2 turntable piece

What can this robot's arm do?

This arm is used for cutting

Plate keeps this robot upright

How to play

1 Each builder gets a handful of bricks and makes a robot.

2 When everyone is finished building, each model maker shares their robot's name, job, and where they are from.

TOP TIP
Give your robot a face using printed eye tiles. The tiles attach to any stud—and you can put your robot's eyes wherever you like.

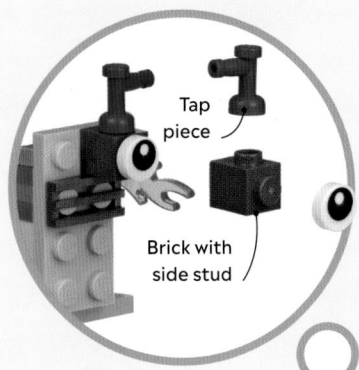

Tap piece

Brick with side stud

Megaphone makes announcements

1x1 cone makes a leg

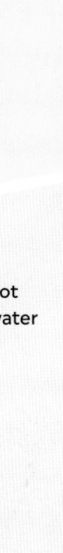

This robot sprays water

Mouth is a 1x2 grille

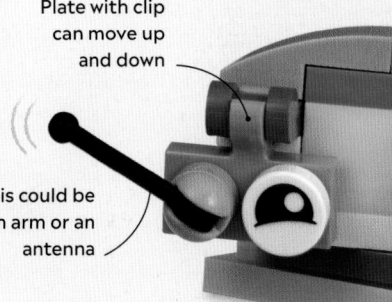

Plate with clip can move up and down

This could be an arm or an antenna

TANGRAM TEASER

Shape up your building skills with a tangram challenge. A tangram is a puzzle that's made from a square that's "cut" into seven shapes—five triangles, a square, and a rhomboid. The pieces can be rearranged to make hundreds of cool pictures. What will you create?

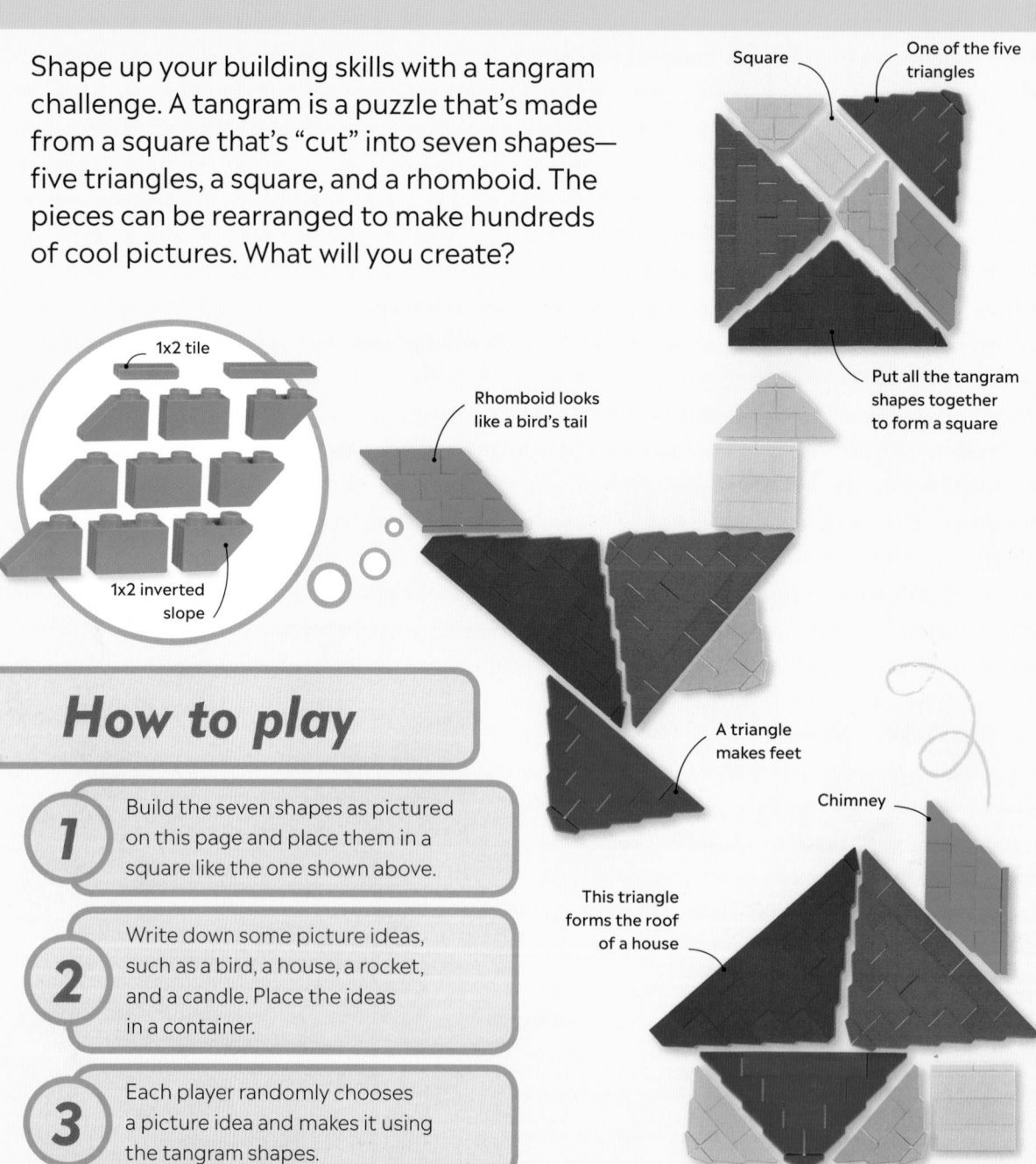

Square

One of the five triangles

Put all the tangram shapes together to form a square

1x2 tile

1x2 inverted slope

Rhomboid looks like a bird's tail

A triangle makes feet

Chimney

This triangle forms the roof of a house

How to play

1 Build the seven shapes as pictured on this page and place them in a square like the one shown above.

2 Write down some picture ideas, such as a bird, a house, a rocket, and a candle. Place the ideas in a container.

3 Each player randomly chooses a picture idea and makes it using the tangram shapes.

CRACK THE CODE

How to play

Invent your own LEGO code and write secret messages for your friends to guess. Who will be the master LEGO code breaker?

1 Build a code board with 26 spaces—one for each letter of the alphabet. Then fill the spaces with an element to represent each letter.

2 Think of a secret message and use the pieces to spell it out.

3 Challenge a friend to decode the message.

Dogs stand for the letter "d"

TOP TIP
Each letter of the alphabet is a different LEGO element. Choose any pieces you want—just be sure that no two letters use the same piece.

Stack bricks on a large baseplate to make each letter space

Can you read the code above? Check the answer on this page.

BUILD BIG THINGS, SMALL

There's nothing like making a big model with lots of LEGO bricks. But can you recreate something that's big in real life—like a tractor, a bus, or a truck—with just a few LEGO elements?

Yellow tiles make the school bus instantly recognizable

A single tile makes a roof

Small slopes make a good hood

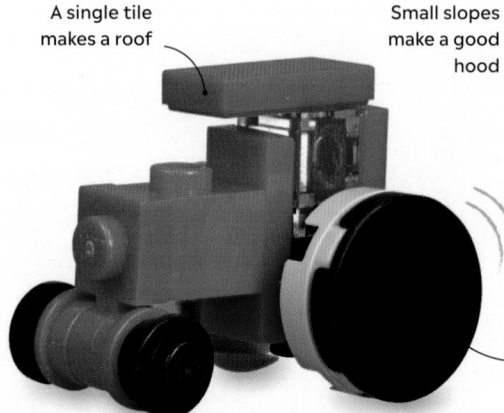

1x1 round plate for a tire

2x2 round tile makes a big tractor tire

TOP TIP

Keep your micro builds to scale by using small LEGO elements, such as 1x1 round plates and 1x2 tiles.

How to build

2x2 plate with pin hole

1x1 round plate

LEGO® Technic half pin

1x2 tile makes a smooth car roof

2 Build the body of the car next. A plate connects the two wheel sections.

1x1 slope makes a rear spoiler

1 To build micro vehicles like this one, start with two plates with pin holes. Then build from the bottom up.

3 Add transparent pieces for windows and slopes and tiles for extra detail.

2x4 plate holds the bottom together

SPECIAL BRICK

This LEGO Technic half pin helps make wheels on all of the mini vehicles pictured here. 1x1 round plates slot onto the pins to make tires.

How to play

1 Choose a category of objects that are big in real life, such as vehicles or animals.

2 Everyone chooses one object within the category to build. For example, if the theme is vehicles, you could build a tractor.

3 Make a micro-scale model of the object using just a handful of LEGO pieces.

It's fine to show studs on top

1x1 plate with rounded top

Slope brick looks like a car hood

Plate with bar fits into a plate with clip so the ladder can move up and down

Red and blue transparent tiles look like emergency lights

Transparent pieces make car windows

YOU'RE ON A ROLL!

BINGO BRICKS

Build bingo boards and grab some friends to play. You'll want to be the first person to mark off three boxes in a row on your board so that you can yell "bingo!" and win the game.

2x2 jumper plates hold each token

Make nine boxes on each board

Stack marks a token that has been called out and matched

B-I-N-G-O!

16x16 baseplate

Make the box borders with any pieces and colors you like

How to play

1 Build the boards and some mini models to use as bingo tokens. Make sure you have plenty of each token before you start the game.

2 Set nine tokens on each player's board, making sure that no two boards are identical. Place the rest of the tokens into a bag.

3 Have one player pull the tokens out of the bag and call them out. If a player has a matching token, they mark it with a stack of bricks.

4 The first person to mark off a row of three in any direction shouts "bingo" and wins the game.

KIDS VS. ADULTS

Imagine who would win in a building face-off between kids and grown-ups. In this challenge, the most creative model comes out on top.

Make steam with white plates

2x2 round plate

2x2 round brick

2x2x2 cone

Chimney

How to play

1 Form teams. One group is for adults and the other for children.

2 Decide what model to make, such as a train.

3 Each team builds the chosen model. Whichever team makes the most creative model wins!

Kids' train

VS.

Adults' train

1x1 round plates are train lights

Rolling wheels

TOP TIP

Think about how an element can become something else. For example, this train uses flowers for wheels and cupcakes for lights.

DO A DOUBLE TAKE

Trick your friends with these baffling builds! These optical illusions make the brain think it is seeing something it is not. But everything becomes clear when you look at the models from a different angle. There's more to these builds than meets the eye!

From the front, this brick hides the back stack to create the optical illusion

Is this brick at the front or back?

Stack does not attach to the horizontal brick, even though it looks like it does!

Open door

From the front, this model looks like a doorway. But look closer and see that the stack of bricks on the right is actually behind the minifigure. The stacks of bricks are two separate structures, connected only by your eyes.

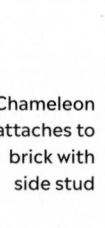

Chameleon attaches to brick with side stud

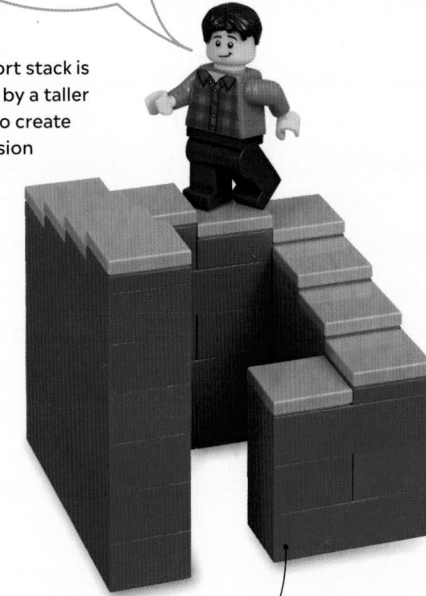

WHERE DOES THIS STAIRCASE LEAD TO?

The short stack is hidden by a taller tower to create the illusion

This stack isn't actually connected to the other side of the model

Never-ending staircase

This minifigure looks like he will be running around in circles forever! But look at the image on the right to see that the staircase does have an end.

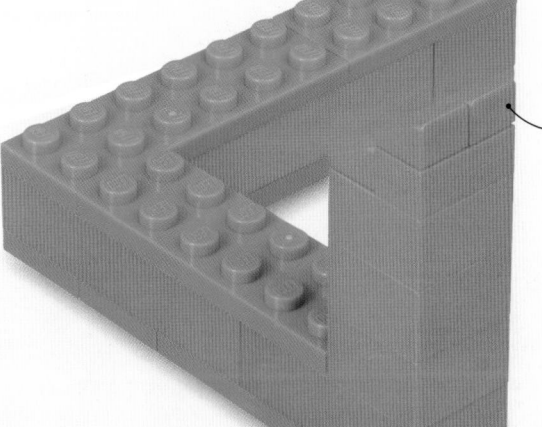

Slopes look like they join to the orange corner

Try this triangle

When you look at the picture on the left, the model looks like a triangle. From a different angle, however, you can see that the build isn't a triangle at all!

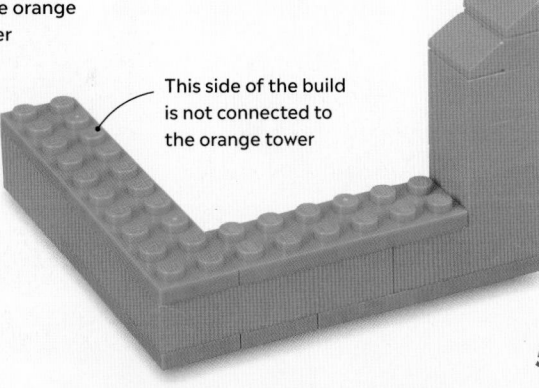

This side of the build is not connected to the orange tower

SLIPPERY STACKS

LEGO bricks were never meant to be stacked on their sides like this! Building this way makes for a very slippy, unstable tower—but it makes for a great game! With 10 seconds to play, will you be able to build a tower and keep it standing?

TOP TIP

Sort your bricks into piles by size before you play. It will make stacking quicker because you won't have to sort as you go.

The wider the brick, the more stable the tower

How to play

1 Set a timer for 10 seconds and stack as many bricks on their sides as you can. You can stack on the long or short side of the bricks.

2 If your tower falls down while you're building, start again.

3 Whoever has the tallest tower that's still standing after the clock stops wins the challenge.

Towers made with all the same size bricks are more stable

Play with any size bricks

How high will your tower be?

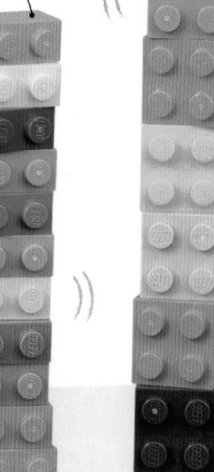
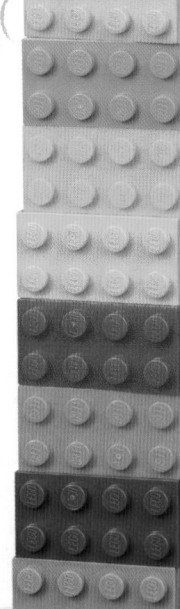

PICTURE THIS!

Grab a LEGO minifigure and a camera. Then recreate a life-size scene at minifigure scale and snap some photos. Who will create the best-looking picture?

THIS GAME IS A SNAP.

EXPLORING THE WILD

How to play

1 Choose a minifigure and think of a scene you want to create, such as walking through the jungle or climbing a mountain.

2 Set up your minifigure in the scene and take a picture. No one's hands can be in the photo.

3 Take a vote at the end to decide who wins the photo challenge.

FAMILY TRIP TO LONDON

TOURING A CASTLE

ARTIST AT A MUSEUM

STRING IT ALONG

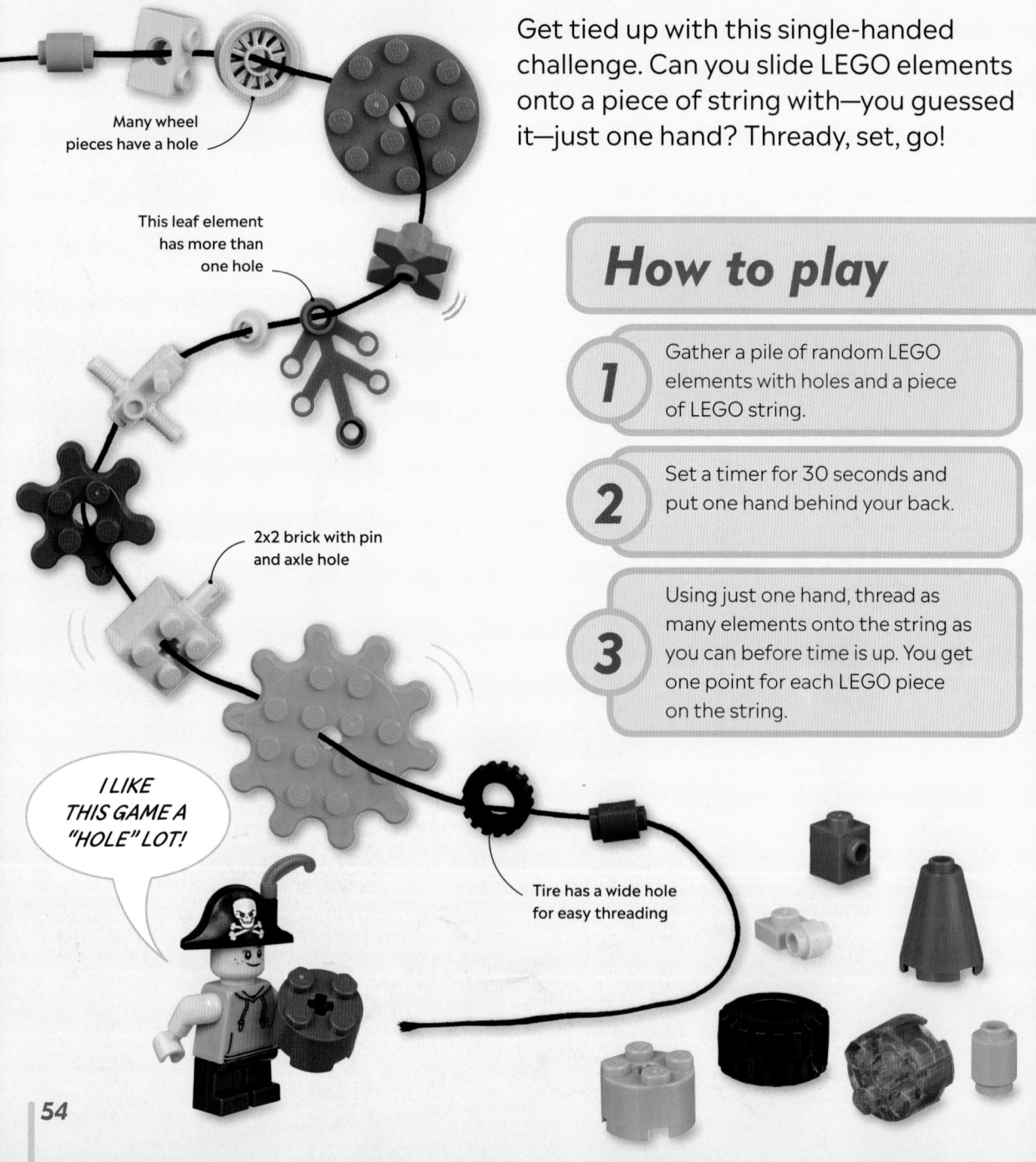

Get tied up with this single-handed challenge. Can you slide LEGO elements onto a piece of string with—you guessed it—just one hand? Thready, set, go!

Many wheel pieces have a hole

This leaf element has more than one hole

2x2 brick with pin and axle hole

I LIKE THIS GAME A "HOLE" LOT!

Tire has a wide hole for easy threading

How to play

1 Gather a pile of random LEGO elements with holes and a piece of LEGO string.

2 Set a timer for 30 seconds and put one hand behind your back.

3 Using just one hand, thread as many elements onto the string as you can before time is up. You get one point for each LEGO piece on the string.

GIVE ME FIVE!

Line up for a game of fivers! Have fun making this board game to play with family and friends. Think ahead to make sure you're the first to get five of your game pieces in a row.

How to play

1 Make your board. Player one gets 10 round bricks in one color, and player two receives 10 in a different color.

2 The aim of the game is to create an unbroken row of five round bricks in one color. The players take turns to place one piece at a time.

3 Each player uses their pieces to try to block their opponent from getting five in a row before they do. The first person to get five in a row wins!

1x1 round plate

Rows can be diagonal, horizontal, or vertical

Use your pieces to block your opponent

Use any bricks to make a border for the game board

FIVE IN A ROW—I WIN!

1x1 round brick

16x16 baseplate

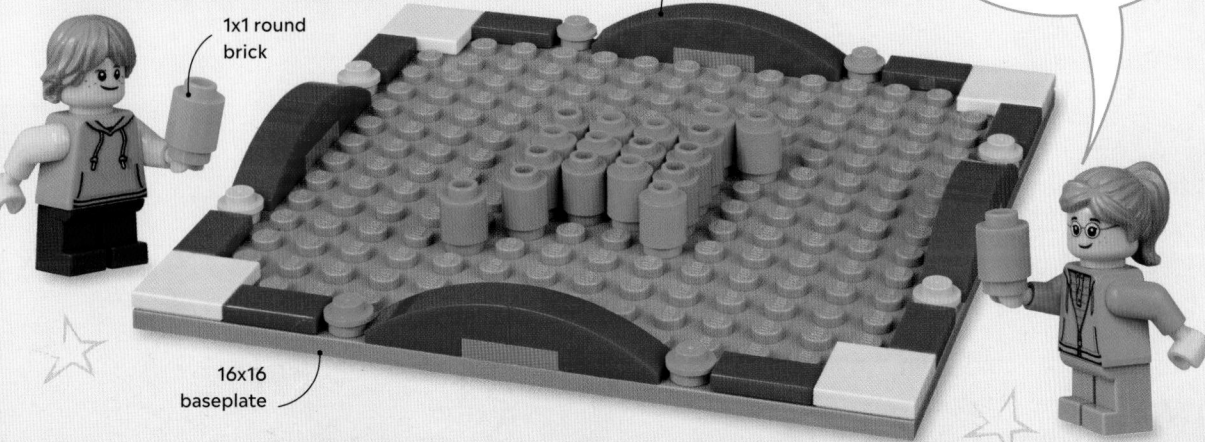

SORT-A-THON

Why not make tidying your LEGO bricks into a game? You can sort your bricks by color, type, size, or shape. Whichever sort of sorter you are, try to beat the clock!

Group by type like these 1x2 bricks

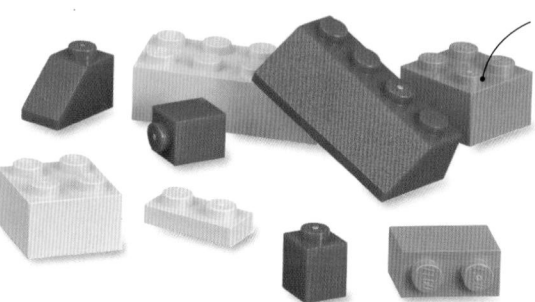

These bricks are sorted by color

Level up

If you're sorting by size or shape, make it trickier by wearing a blindfold. Use your hands to feel the shape of your bricks, or count the studs to sort by size.

How to play

1 Decide what types of piles to sort your bricks into. You can do it by shape, size, type, or color.

2 Set a timer for 20 seconds.

3 Whoever sorts their piles correctly before time is up is the winner.

I SORT OF HAVE THE HANG OF IT!

SUPER SURPRISES

What could you create with your eyes closed? You can build anything at all. The only rule is that you can't look at what you're making until the timer goes off. Build yourself a surprise!

TOP TIP
Arrange your bricks in a clear space before you put on your blindfold. This way you'll have everything you need right in front of you.

Maybe you'll make a silly robot like this one

Which way is up? You won't be able to tell when blindfolded

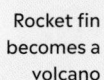

Rocket fin becomes a volcano

Double inverted slope makes a body

This plate looks like an alien's dress

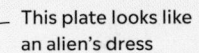

How to play

1 Give each player a handful of bricks and a blindfold.

2 Set a timer for one minute and build with your blindfolds on.

3 When time is up, take a look at your builds and guess what each person has made.

HOW'S IT LOOKING?

This looks like it could be an air horn

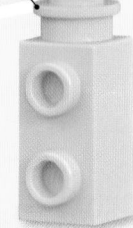

SLIDING SQUARES

It takes patience to beat this brick-built sliding puzzle. Decorate the sliding squares with a picture before mixing it all up. Then time yourself to see how long it takes you to solve it.

You can choose any colors for your border

How to build

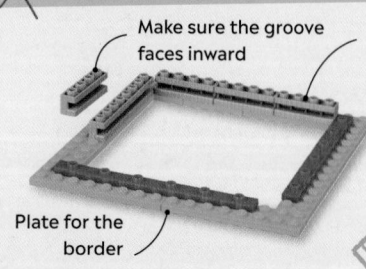

Make sure the groove faces inward

1x4 slider brick with groove

Plate for the border

1 Use plates to make a square. Add slider bricks to two sides of the square.

2 Fit some of the sliding squares into the slider bricks.

Sliding square

Plate adds height for slide plates

Slide plate

3 Place slide plates along the other two edges.

58

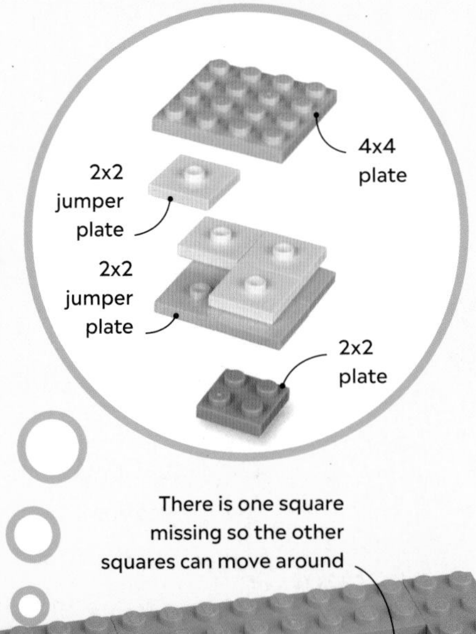

2x2 jumper plate

4x4 plate

2x2 jumper plate

2x2 plate

SPECIAL BRICKS

These slider bricks and slide plates have grooves on one side. These pieces hold the squares in the frame and let them move around.

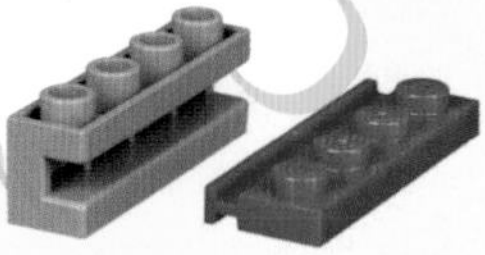

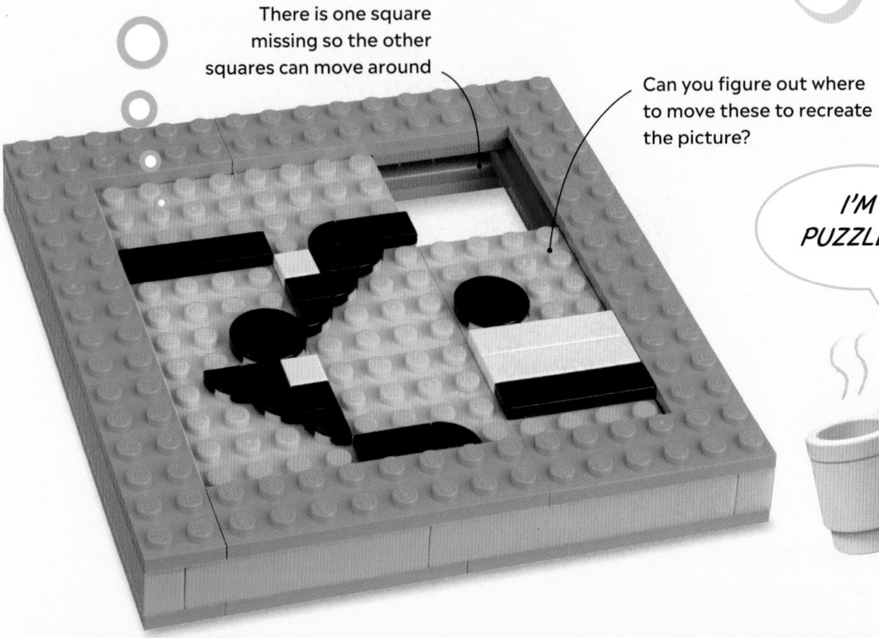

There is one square missing so the other squares can move around

Can you figure out where to move these to recreate the picture?

I'M PUZZLED!

4 Insert the rest of the squares. Add bricks that are one brick high and one brick wide to form a border around the slider bricks and slide plates.

2x8 plate

There will be a gap one square wide

5 Your puzzle is ready to decorate.

MINIFIGURE MIX-UP

Have you ever met an astronaut-mermaid or hugged a minotaur-teddy bear? Well, now you can! Mix up your minifigures in this fun game and try to put them back together correctly without looking. You might end up with some interesting new characters!

How to play

1 Take apart your minifigures and set them on a flat surface. Mix them up with your hands.

2 Put on a blindfold and try to piece each minifigure back together.

3 When all the pieces are connected again, take off your blindfold. Are your minifigures matching?

SOMETHING LOOKS FISHY...

GIVE ME SOME SPACE!

WHERE ARE MY LEGS?

NOT-MY-ARMS CHALLENGE

In this game, you can play with your eyes or your hands, but not both! Can you and a friend work together to make a model like these with only one set of eyes and one pair of arms? Lend a friend a hand or two to build something fun.

ARE THESE MY ARMS?

Slopes make duck feet

TOP TIP
The player that can see the bricks can give the second player directions—they just can't use their hands or arms to help build the model.

Wedge plate attaches to bricks with side studs

Curved slope makes a robot arm

Building on a baseplate keeps the model steady

How to play

1 Set out a pile of bricks on a flat surface.

2 One player sits down with their hands behind their back. The other player stands behind them and slips their arms under the first player's arms. Just the first player can see the bricks.

3 The first player tells the second player what to build. Only the second player can use their hands and arms to make the model.

IMPOSSIBLE PUZZLE

Believe it or not, these rectangles can come apart without breaking the whole puzzle! But will any of your family and friends be able to figure out how it's done?

Make each puzzle piece in a different color so the brainteaser is easier to solve

SPECIAL BRICK

Tiles like this 2x4 tile allow the build to slide apart. Each piece needs a smooth finish so it doesn't get stuck to another piece.

Which piece slides off first?

How to build

1 Each puzzle piece is built the same apart from one, which has closed-up sides.

1x6 plate

2x4 plate

2x4 plate

1x3 plate

2 Hold the base layer of plates together with bricks.

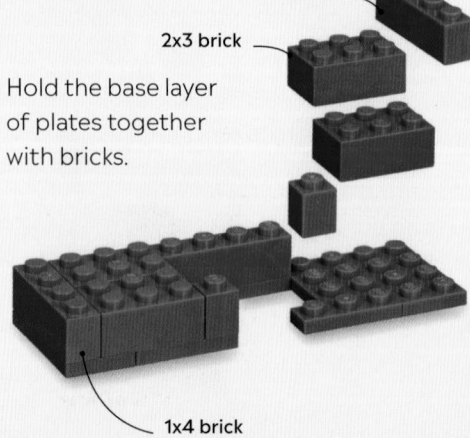

1x4 brick

2x3 brick

1x4 brick

How to play

3 Move the yellow puzzle piece down so that it rests inside the green puzzle piece.

Slide this piece down

1 Slide a bit of one puzzle piece with a gap through the piece with closed sides. Don't push it all the way in.

Gap should face up

Puzzle piece with closed sides

4 Slide the green piece through the red one so that all the pieces connect in the middle. Then challenge your friends to take it apart.

Push this piece through the part with closed sides

Gap is here

2 Place the other puzzle piece with a gap on top of the piece with closed sides. Gently slide the piece downward.

Make sure this piece isn't pushed in too far

One piece has two closed sides

1x6 brick

3 Cover the bricks with tiles so that the puzzle pieces do not stick together.

2x2 tile

2x4 tile

1x2 tile

Leave an opening on two of the puzzle pieces

4 Two of the puzzle pieces need a gap in one side. The third should be closed on all sides to form a hole in the middle.

63

READY, SET, THROW!

How many points can you rack up with a handful of elements and a brick-built frame? Simply stand behind the toss line and gently throw your bricks into the frame. Aim for inside the centermost ring to score the most points!

How to play

1 Build a frame with three rings. The smaller the ring, the more points scored.

2 Set the board on a flat surface and take five steps back. Mark the "toss line" with a brick so everyone stands in the same place.

3 Everyone gets five bricks to throw into the frame. Whoever earns the most points wins.

Tossing a brick in the center earns five points

Bricks tossed in the outside ring are worth one point each

Wall is one brick high

Level up

Why not challenge yourself by facing away from the game board and tossing bricks over your shoulder? Just make sure no one is standing nearby!

Earn 2 points by landing in the middle ring

32x32 plate makes a good base for the frame

COLLAB BUILD

Great minds think alike . . . or do they?
Take turns with a friend to build a
model, one LEGO element at a time.
How similar—or different—will your
building styles be?

How to play

1 With one friend or more,
decide what object you
want to build together.

2 Take turns to add
just one brick at a
time. What will the
model look like when
you're finished?

Would your
castle have a
flame piece?

TOP TIP
Don't rush to add your
next brick. Wait to see what
gets added to the model
before you choose what
piece you'll put on next.

1x1 flower
element

Textured brick
looks like a
castle wall

*I'M ROYALLY
IMPRESSED!*

SPOT THE DIFFERENCE

Do you have an eye for details? Use your eagle eyes to spot the difference between two 3-D scenes. You can play this game again and again by changing around the elements each time—or building entirely new scenes.

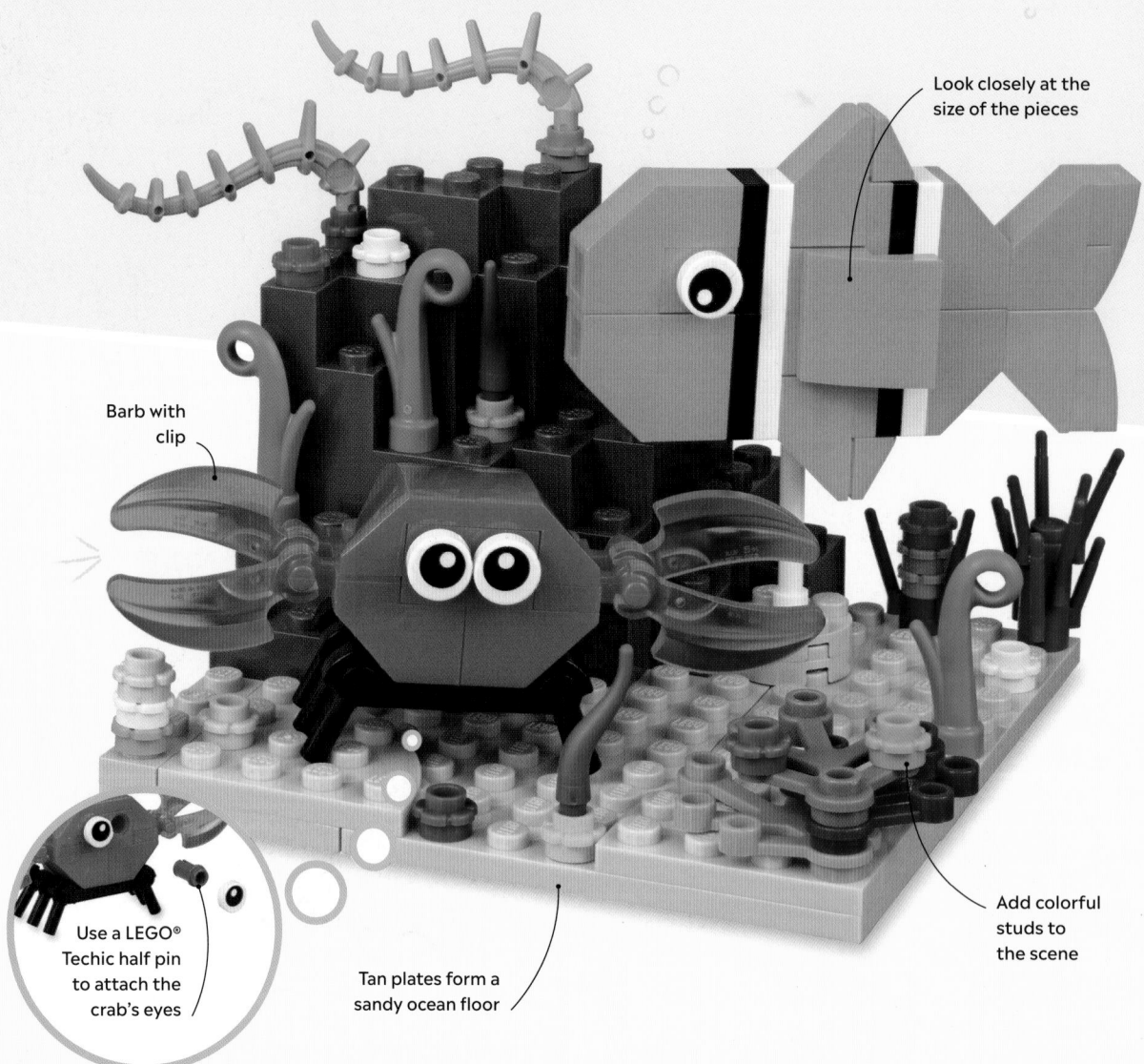

Look closely at the size of the pieces

Barb with clip

Use a LEGO® Techic half pin to attach the crab's eyes

Tan plates form a sandy ocean floor

Add colorful studs to the scene

How to play

1 Build two identical scenes, such as a coral reef like this one.

2 Make changes to one of the scenes, by adding or moving elements.

3 Remember to write down the differences between the scenes!

4 Challenge your friends and family to spot all of the differences.

Plant pieces make floating seagrass

CAN YOU SPOT ALL OF THE DIFFERENCES?

Swapping out colors is an easy way to add a difference

MEMORY CUBE MATCHUP

Put your mind to the test with this memorable game. Make LEGO cards with any patterns or pictures you like, and cover them up with specially built cubes. Who will be the best match maker?

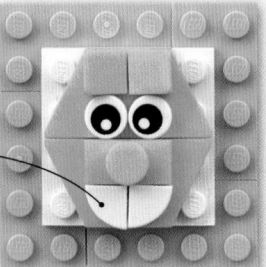

Use any small elements to create your own picture or design

Cool cards

You'll need to choose six different patterns or pictures to put on your cards. Build two identical LEGO cards for each design. These cards have cute faces, but you can make anything you want.

How to build

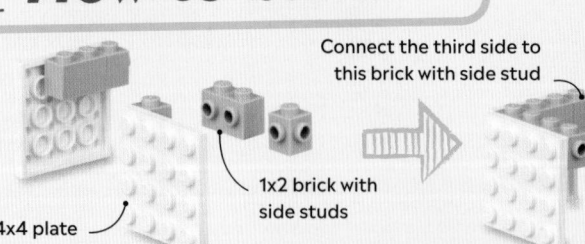
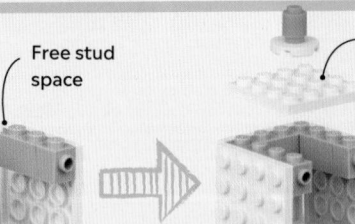

Connect the third side to this brick with side stud

Free stud space

Fifth 4x4 plate makes the top of the cube

1x2 brick with side studs

1x2 brick with side studs

4x4 plate

1 Fix bricks with side studs along the top edges of two 4x4 plates. Connect the plates using the bricks with side studs.

2 Repeat with a third 4x4 plate so that the cube has three sides.

3 Add a fourth plate with a 1x2 brick with side studs. Place a final plate on top and add a round brick on a jumper plate for a "handle."

How to play

1 Build six pairs of cards. Build 12 cubes to hide the squares.

2 Mix the cube-covered cards and line them up in rows.

3 Each person takes a turn to choose two cubes. Lift each cube to reveal the cards beneath. If the two cards match, the player keeps them. If they don't, then the two cards are covered up again.

4 Whoever has the most pairs at the end of the game wins.

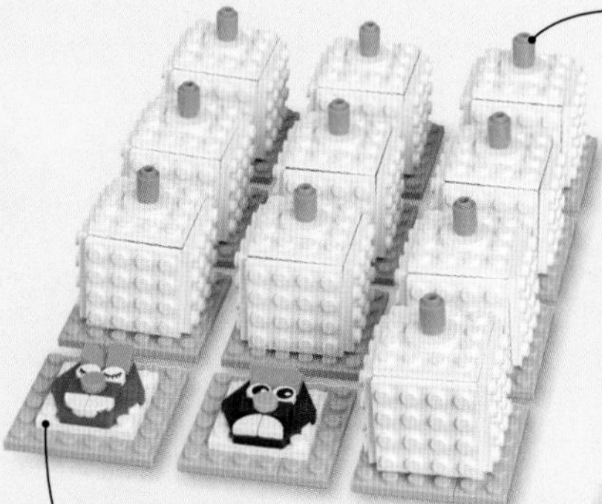

1x1 round bricks should be the same color on all cubes

The squares do not match so need to be covered up again

YOU CAN'T OUTFOX ME!

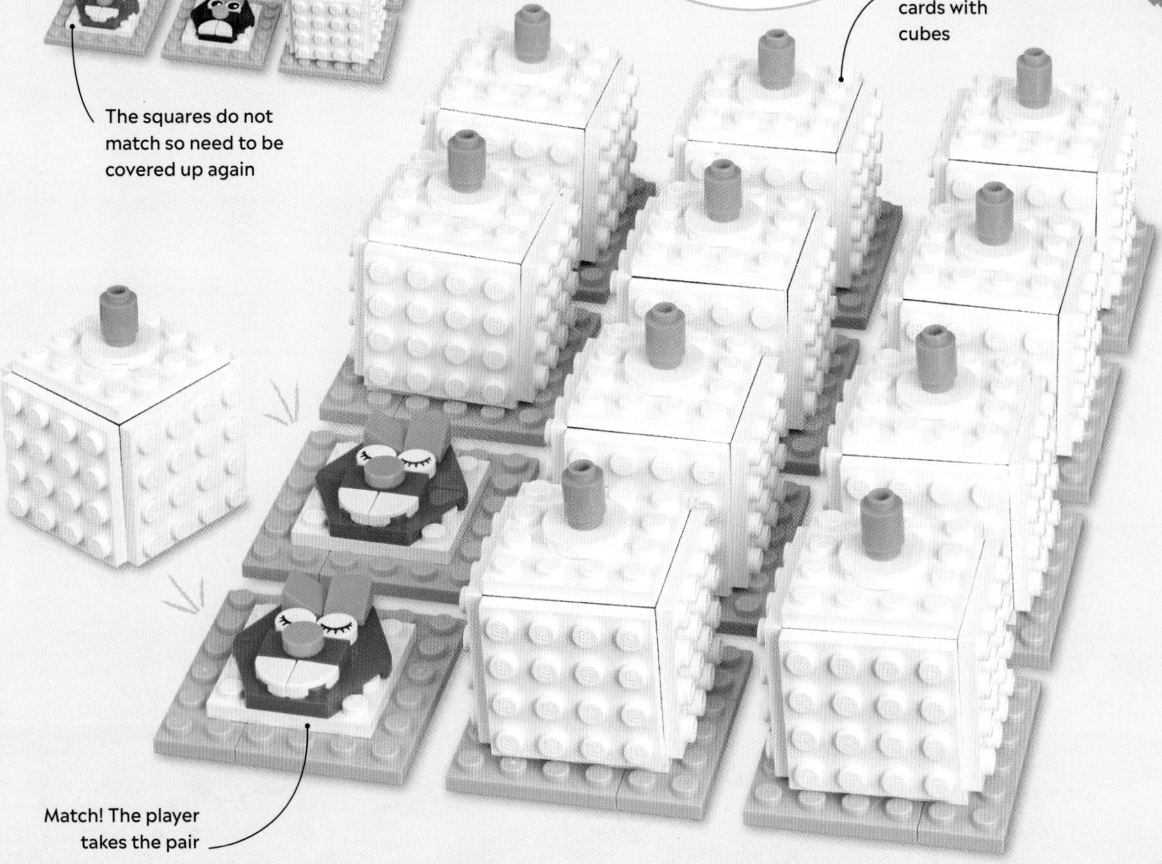

Cover up the cards with cubes

Match! The player takes the pair

DOMINO CHAIN REACTION

Line 'em up, and knock 'em down! Challenge yourself to create a chain of LEGO dominoes that will all fall down after the first one is pushed. How long can you make your chain?

THIS GAME IS BANANAS!

Space the dominoes close enough so they knock into each other when they fall

How to play

1 Build your dominoes. Stand your dominoes one in front of the other to create as long a line as you can.

2 When you have finished making your chain, gently knock over the first domino. The goal is for each domino to fall over once you set off the chain reaction.

3 If the chain reaction stops before it reaches the last domino, you lose the game.

Each domino is the same size so the chain reaction will work

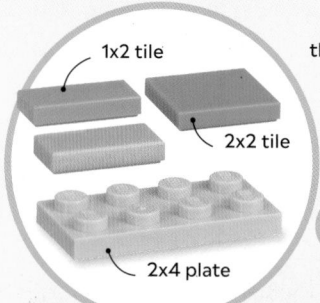

1x2 tile

2x2 tile

2x4 plate

The base of each block is a 2x4 plate

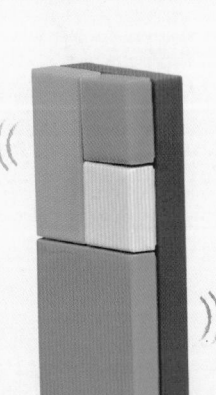

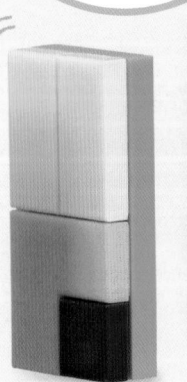

Cover the plates with any size and color tiles

DON'T PICK THAT BRICK!

Need a way to decide whose turn it is to do the dishes? Try your luck with this game of chance! All you need is a container and an assortment of LEGO bricks in two different colors, plus one piece in a third color. Take turns to see who will pick out the odd brick—good luck!

BEST OF THREE?

You can use any container, but a nontransparent one makes sure no one can peek!

How to play

1 Fill a container with two different colors of LEGO pieces. Add one brick in a third color and shake up the container to mix the bricks.

The pink brick is the "odd" brick

2 Pass the container around a group. Each person closes their eyes and chooses a brick. If someone chooses the "odd" brick, they lose the game.

Choosing a green brick means you're still in the game

Yellow bricks are safe to choose

SPY MISSION

Have you ever dreamed of being a spy? This game tests your snooping skills! The player who is chosen to be the spy must look at what another team is building and report back to their team. Will your team be able to copy what the opposing team is building in just 15 minutes?

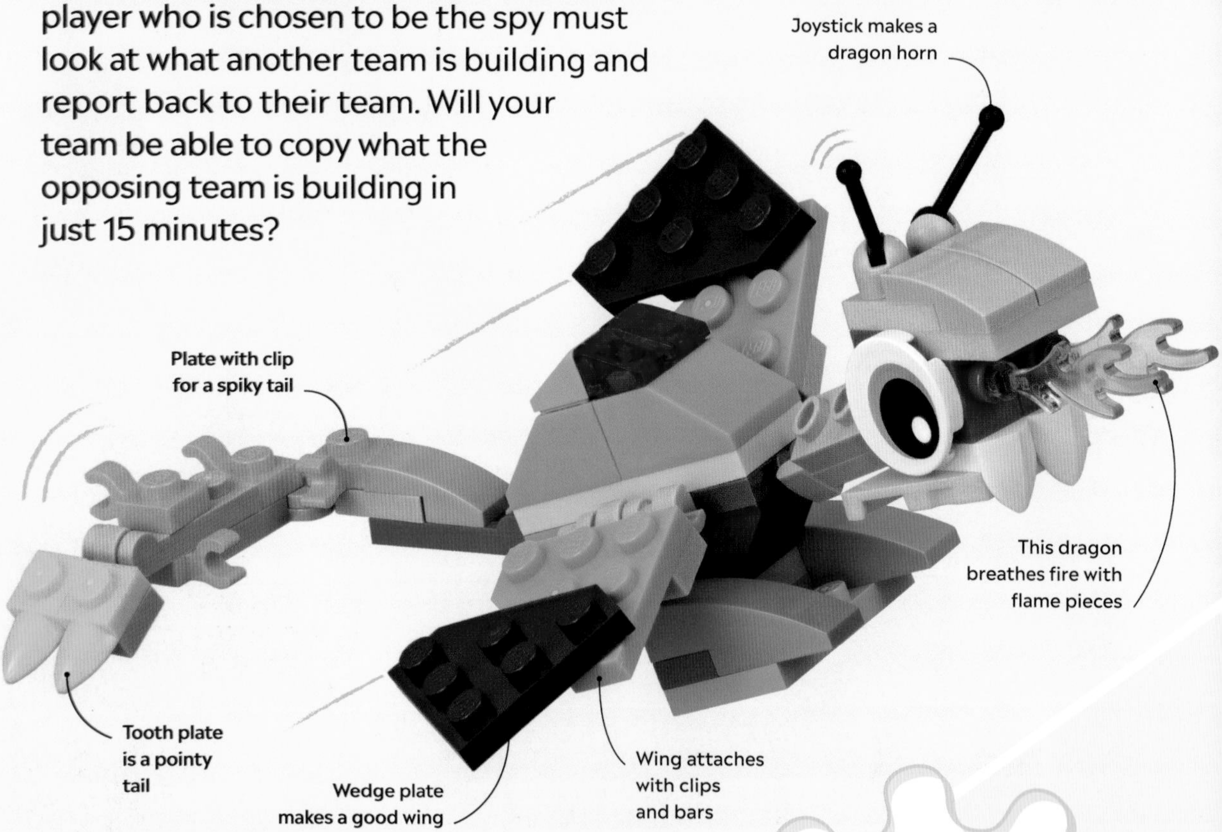

Joystick makes a dragon horn

Plate with clip for a spiky tail

This dragon breathes fire with flame pieces

Tooth plate is a pointy tail

Wedge plate makes a good wing

Wing attaches with clips and bars

I SPY A FIRE-BREATHING DRAGON!

TOP TIP
Spies can't take photos of the other team's model. But they can take notes and draw pictures of what they see to share with their team.

72

How to play

1 Form two teams of two people or more.

2 Each team gets a pile of identical LEGO elements in separate areas so each team cannot see what the other is building.

3 Set a timer for 15 minutes. One team starts building a model. The other team picks one person to be the spy.

4 The spy checks what the model-making team is building and reports back to their own team. Spies cannot build and cannot speak to the other team. The model-making team cannot speak to the spy.

5 After 15 minutes, compare models. The spy team gets a point if their build is similar to the model-making team's build. Play again, swapping the spy team each time.

VS.

This team used flame pieces for ears

Both teams have eyes in the same place

Tooth plate for fierce fangs

Ball joint connects the wing on this dragon

Plate with clip holds the legs

1x1 tooth plate makes a talon

I'M "DRAGON" SOME CLUES BACK TO MY TEAM.

MYSTERY MAKER

Could you build a model without knowing what you're supposed to be making? Take the challenge and find out whether you can build a mystery model!

How to play

1 Set out a pile of simple bricks. One player will be the director. The director decides what the other player will build but doesn't share the model idea with the builder.

2 The builder follows the director's instructions until the model is complete. Will the builder be able to make the correct model?

1x2 brick makes the camel's hump

Darker brick looks like a hoof

THIS IS A REAL MYSTERY!

Is this model going to be a robot or an alien?

Level up

It's trickier to build models with lots of different kinds of pieces. Set out an assortment of LEGO elements to make the game more challenging.

1x1 cone

BRICK GALLERY

All LEGO® bricks are useful, and some are especially helpful for creating games and challenges. Don't worry if you don't have all of these parts. Get creative with the pieces you do have.

Brick basics

Bricks are the basis of most LEGO builds. They come in many shapes and sizes and are named according to size. Plates are the same as bricks, only slimmer. Three stacked plates are the same height as a standard brick.

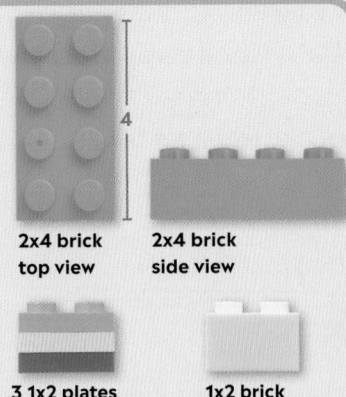

2x4 brick top view

2x4 brick side view

3 1x2 plates

1x2 brick

Tiles

Tiles look like plates, but without any studs on top. This gives them a smooth look for more realistic builds.

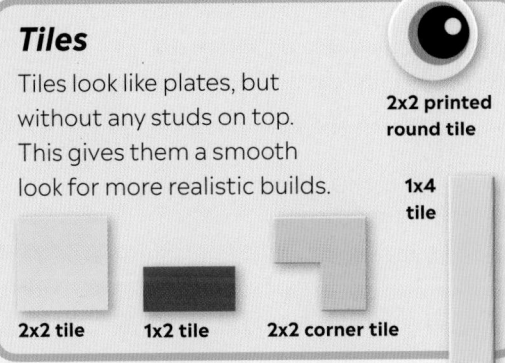

2x2 printed round tile

1x4 tile

2x2 tile

1x2 tile

2x2 corner tile

Slopes

Slopes are any bricks with diagonal angles. They can be big, small, curved, or inverted (upside-down).

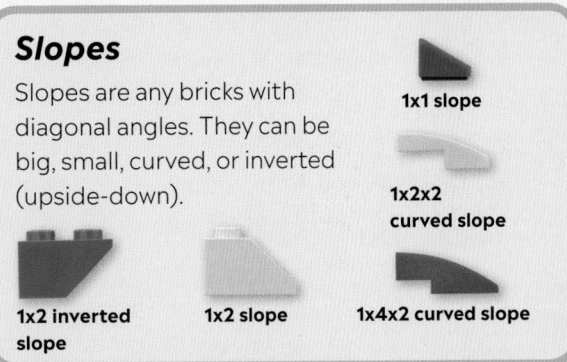

1x1 slope

1x2x2 curved slope

1x2 inverted slope

1x2 slope

1x4x2 curved slope

Cool connectors

Bricks don't have to be stacked. Connect elements in different ways using some of these pieces.

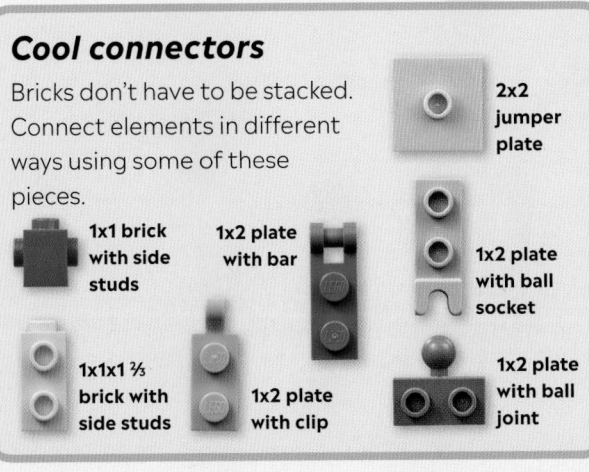

1x1 brick with side studs

1x2 plate with bar

1x1x1 ⅔ brick with side studs

1x2 plate with clip

2x2 jumper plate

1x2 plate with ball socket

1x2 plate with ball joint

Special pieces

Get creative with all types of LEGO pieces. These elements are great for completing challenges and games as well as decorating builds.

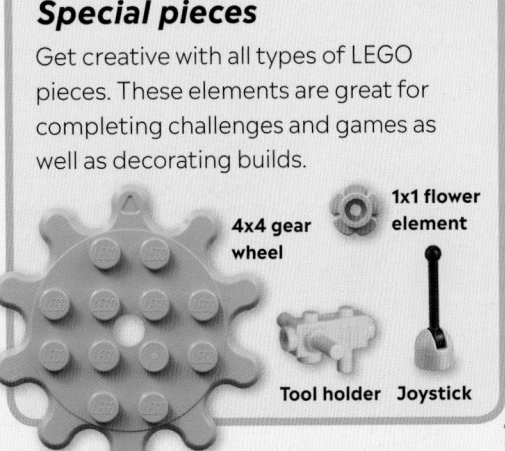

4x4 gear wheel

1x1 flower element

Tool holder

Joystick

DK | Penguin Random House

Senior Editor Tori Kosara
Senior Designer Anna Formanek
Designer James McKeag
Production Editor Siu Yin Chan
Senior Production Controller Louise Daly
Managing Editor Paula Regan
Managing Art Editor Jo Connor
Art Director Lisa Lanzarini
Publisher Julie Ferris
Publishing Director Mark Searle

Inspirational models built by
Alice Finch, A. Formanek, Rod Gillies,
Steve Guinness, Tori Kosara, James McKeag,
and Barney Main

Photography by Gary Ombler

Dorling Kindersley would like to thank
Randi Sørensen, Heidi K. Jensen, Paul Hansford,
Martin Leighton Lindhardt, Nina Koopman, and
Charlotte Neidhardt at the LEGO Group; Jenny
Edwards, Rosie Peet, and Nicole Reynolds at
DK; and Jennette ElNaggar for proofreading.

First American Edition, 2020
Published in the United States by
DK Publishing
1450 Broadway, Suite 801, New York, NY 10018

Page design copyright © 2020 Dorling
Kindersley Limited

DK, a Division of Penguin Random House LLC
20 21 22 23 24 10 9 8 7 6 5 4 3 2 1
001–316405–Sep/2020

Manufactured by DK, One Embassy Gardens,
8 Viaduct Gardens, London SW11 7BW
under license from the LEGO Group.

A catalog record for this book
is available from the Library of Congress.
ISBN 978-1-4654-9786-4
978-0-7440-2428-9 (library edition)

Printed and bound in China

For the curious

www.dk.com
www.LEGO.com

Meet the builders

Steve Guinness

Steve Guinness dreams in LEGO®
bricks and loves building with his
LEGO collection. Steve thinks
that playing with LEGO
bricks should always be fun,
which is why he really enjoyed
building the funny face mask for
the "Try not to laugh" challenge.

James McKeag

LEGO fan James particularly
enjoyed building "Escape the
maze" with its colorful walls.
James's top tip for building with
LEGO bricks is to be as creative as
possible. Your models won't always
look the way you imagined them,
and that's okay!